Canadian Bread
Machine Baking
with Roxanne McQuilkin

Canadian Bread Machine Baking

with Roxanne McQuilkin

Macmillan Canada
Toronto

Canadian Cataloguing in Publication Data
McQuilkin, Roxanne
  Canadian bread machine baking with Roxanne McQuilkin

Includes index.
ISBN 0-7715-7390-1
1. Bread. 2. Automatic bread machines. I. Title.
TX769.M3 1996   641.8'15   C96-930953-8

Macmillan Canada wishes to thank the Canada Council, the Ontario Ministry of Culture and Communications and the Ontario Arts Council for supporting its publishing program.

Cover and text design: Dennis Boyes
Cover photograph: Quebecor Studio

Macmillan Canada
A Division of Canada Publishing Corporation
Toronto, Ontario, Canada

    4 5 TG 00 99 98 97

Printed in Canada

To my husband, Paul Robson,
and to my mother

Acknowledgments

There are some people I thank for their support and counsel. Even before this book was started, thank you Suzanne Bourret of the *Hamilton Spectator*, who saw a need for just such a book, judging by the letters from her readers, and Cynthia David, another food editor who encouraged me to begin the task for the same reason; to Moira who supported my endeavour in many ways and to those who sought my advice.

Sincere appreciation to Paul, who acted as editor and sounding board, to name a few roles husbands fill, and who deserves the dedication of this book, for always being there and giving the extra required.

Special thanks to the following companies for providing samples of their bread machines and expert advice: Panasonic, CharlesCraft, Sanyo, Sunbeam. Thanks also to Black and Decker, Hitachi, Regal, and Gemini Packaging (Ferma Pan) for their expert assistance.

Other brands of bread machines were also used and I appreciate my friends for their loan.

Thanks to the bread testers and recipe testers: most of my friends who live near by, my neighbours on Clendenan Avenue, my neighbours on Marttila Drive, the Patrzaleks, the Maynards, Heather Mackey & Associates, Lynda Boyd.

Thanks to Macmillan Canada staff whose talents show in every letter and space herein. Special thanks to Denise Schon for giving the start and Kirsten Hanson for making my ideas into reality.

Contents

4
Using This Book

5
Loaves

6
Hand-Shaped Breads and Rolls

Preface

A bread machine of your very own is convenient hedonism. Imagine butter melting decadently over a thick slice of fresh warm bread or awakening to the rich yeasty aroma of a baking loaf.

In just a few years, the automatic bread maker has become one of the standard kitchen appliances used on a regular basis in many Canadian homes. Still, its use has been limited by a number of factors.

Most bread machines have been made in Asia, using local measures, local ingredients and recipes developed for their native tastes. When these machines are exported to North America, some manufacturers simply translate the recipe books to English.

Flour varies throughout North America and amounts in your bread machine cookbook may have been converted into US measures for that market and then reconverted into metric for the Canadian market, hence compounding any error. So if the recipes in your instruction manual do not work as well as they should, this is probably why.

While these manuals are useful in telling you how to use your bread machine, many of the recipes are not appropriate for Canadian kitchens.

That is why I decided to write this book. All the recipes have been tested using Canadian flour and the quantities are the actual quantities that I used in the testing, not a double conversion.

I have included information on the chemistry of bread making so that whether you are high and dry in the mountains of Alberta or low and moist on one of our sea coasts, you can make intelligent decisions about how to make good bread consistently into great bread.

One of the first automatic bread machines available in Canada was developed by Matsushita Electric Limited of Japan and introduced to the Canadian market in 1989 under the Panasonic brand name. As Matsushita's national home economist at the time, I worked closely with the technicians in Japan to develop the first Canadian instruction manuals and recipe books.

As other manufacturers brought their bread machines onto the Canadian market, I evaluated them and compared their performance.

While all the machines made nice fresh bread, I found that in most cases the recipe books were limited in their information and had not been properly adapted to Canadian ingredients, measures and tastes.

In all my research and my conversations with bread machine owners I found one common theme: people loved their bread machines and wanted to do more with them.

Few Canadians are familiar with the technical aspects of making yeast products. The instruction manuals and recipe books that come with bread machines are sometimes confusing. They do not address many of the important factors that are unique to Canadian bread making and do not explain the chemical and technical processes that are key to the successful baking of yeast products.

We are fortunate in Canada to grow the very best wheat in the world and our milling companies make some of the very finest flour in the world. As with all other types of cooking, the right ingredients in the right quantities are the secret to creating great results.

This book enables Canadian bread bakers to understand how their machine works and why it is important to use recipes developed here in Canada. As a Canadian home economist who has worked with automatic bread machines since they were first brought into the country, I have developed these more than 100 recipes using ingredients that are available throughout Canada.

These recipes will appeal to all Canadians who like to bake and eat breads of all kinds. They will appeal to homemakers who are interested in providing an interesting and wholesome diet, to teenagers who like pizza and bread with pizzazz, to retired men who find challenge and pleasure in honing their bread-making skills. Whether you are a nibbler or a gourmet experimenter, there is plenty here to keep you busy and stimulated.

The book is divided into a number of different sections. The first recipe chapter includes recipes based on all-purpose flour, recipes that use more complex flour mixtures and breads with lots of luscious additions. For those of you with special food needs, I've included special-diet and gluten-free recipes.

There are recipes for hand-shaped rolls, buns, braids and cakes, recipes for snacks, sandwiches, toasts, luncheons, dinners and desserts. All the recipes have been developed in two sizes, to fit any bread machine.

I hope that these recipes, especially designed for Canadian tastes, with Canadian ingredients and Canadian measures, will encourage you to expand your bread-making horizons, branch out and try more exotic flavours and enjoy your bread machine to the fullest.

Chapter One

An Introduction to Automatic Bread Machines

$\mathcal{T}$here are some 15 different bread machine brands on the market in Canada today. All of these machines work on the same principle and have similar programs and construction.

WHAT ARE THEY?

Bread machines are designed to make one loaf of bread from start to finish. The machine warms the ingredients, mixes them, kneads them, lets the dough rise, punches it down and then lets it rise some more. All the while an internal microprocessor controls the heat to give a cosy, warm temperature comfortable for proofing (the technical term for letting the dough rise). Finally, the heat is turned up and the bread is baked. This whole process is accompanied by a wonderful, mouth-watering aroma. Let's look at the machines more closely.

Basically, each machine is surrounded by an attractive outer case where the controls are located. The case protects the interior electronic components and acts as a heat barrier, maintaining the consistent heat level required inside the machine. The outside casing of the bread machine is usually made of plastic and metal. Although the plastic is designed to withstand higher temperatures, the machine should be placed away from other heat sources, especially ovens, stoves, electric kettles and toasters.

The internal temperature of the machine gets quite high when the bread is baking, but it is well insulated from the outer casing so that you will not be burned if you touch the bread machine during baking. The best way to ensure that the bread machine has been properly tested is to check that it has a CSA (Canadian Standards Association) approval sticker.

The microprocessor that controls the mechanical functions, heating, cooling, programming times and other variables is sealed out of sight in the bread machine. Some more sophisticated units monitor the environment to adjust warming temperatures and program periods. This is another reason why you need to select a well-ventilated area for your automatic bread machine away from other sources of heat and cold.

With these sophisticated units, the times for specific programs will change. If you find that the automatic bread machine has modified its program to suit the temperature and humidity in your kitchen, don't worry – your watch is not broken.

When you lift the lid of your automatic bread machine, you will see a removable metal bread pan known as a "bucket." The bucket features its own paddle, known as the "kneading blade." The bucket may have ridges down the side or there may be a removable rod that sticks through the side of the bucket and turns the dough ball in a random pattern during kneading. The interior of the bucket, the paddle and the rod usually have nonstick surfaces, which make them much easier to clean after use.

With the bucket removed, you can see that the interior of the casing is usually made of steel or aluminum. You can also see a number of small protrusions on the interior wall. These are probably the sensors, of which the most important is the thermostat. On some machines some of the protrusions may be the guides that make the pan fit securely and may include sensors that detect if the pan is in place. They may also activate a warning light or prevent the unit from functioning if the pan is not in place. Take great care not to bend or dent them.

When you look down inside an automatic bread machine, you can see the gears, which hold the bread pan and engage the paddle inside the pan, at the bottom of the unit. Always take care to insert the pan correctly so as not to damage them. Some pans require a twist during insertion, while others need a strong push straight down.

Circling the bottom of the unit is a resistance rod, like the heating element in an electric oven. Its function is to heat the bread pan and bake the bread. The heating element is both thermostatically and timer controlled through the internal microprocessor. The element will warm the unit to enable the dough to rise. Then, after the rising time has elapsed, it will increase the heat in order to bake the bread. This rod tends to hold heat, so make sure it has cooled down properly before you touch it. You should also be careful not to bend, scratch or move it.

Size

If your bread machine is rated to make two sizes of pound loaves, then try the large loaf before trying the small size.

HOW THEY WORK

The basic operation is the same in all automatic bread machines. After you have put in all the ingredients, the machine mixes them gently. After this initial mixing, the machine kneads the ingredients more vigorously for a preset period. Then, the thermostatically controlled heating element switches on to warm the dough and help it rise. This usually takes 30 to 40 minutes, depending on the machine. When the dough has risen to about twice its original size, it is kneaded again for a few seconds – this punching down gets rid of any large air spaces that may have developed during rising. Finally the inside of the bread machine heats up to about 425°F (215°C) and bakes the bread for about 40 minutes. Usually the bread machine then signals in some way that the bread is ready. Some machines require that the bread be taken out as soon as baking is finished, while others have a cycle in which they air-cool the loaf before signalling. Then you are able to taste your beautiful, fresh-baked loaf.

Each brand and model of automatic bread machine has its own programming system. Some machines may be programmed to allow for variations in the ingredients, or the size of the loaf, or different degrees of browning on the crust. Most machines can be programmed to delay their start so that the bread is fresh baked when you get up in the morning or come home from work. Other programs can interrupt the process and give you a signal so that you can add ingredients, or remove and use the risen dough for rolls or specialty breads that you want to shape by hand and finish in the oven.

Bread machines come in several sizes and I offer recipes for large and small loaves. Every machine should be able to handle the small loaf recipes, but check your machine before trying the larger quantities, as your machine may be designed for smaller loaves only.

Chapter Two

The Role of Ingredients

$\mathcal{A}$s with any other baking, the quality of the finished product depends to a great extent on the quality of the ingredients. Good-quality fresh ingredients will always give the best results.

FLOURS

Modern milling methods have changed and improved the flours we use for making bread today. Our flour is very different from the flour that pioneers got in the 19th century after taking a huge sack of wheat to the nearest mill. Their coarse flour might have lasted only two or three months before becoming rancid.

You may use a variety of flours in your automatic bread machine. Some may come from wheat and include more or less of the wheat germ; others may come from different varieties of wheats, rye, barley, rice, beans, buckwheat, corn, oats or other grains. Different flours have different characteristics, some of which change over time. Knowing these characteristics enables you to have more consistent quality in your bread baking.

Gluten I

Only wheat and rye flours have naturally occurring gluten. So the other flours cannot be used to make yeast bread unless they are mixed with a wheat or rye flour.

FLOURS WITH GLUTEN

The main difference between the wheat flours used in bread making and those used in other types of baking is that the flour used for bread requires a high gluten content. Gluten helps the dough to stretch and form thin-walled cells or tiny balloons and makes the bread tender.

Chemically, gluten is a protein occurring naturally in wheat and to a lesser extent in other grains. Fresh whole wheat flour and all-purpose white flour have sufficient naturally occurring gluten that you do not need to add gluten. They also have enough gluten for you to add up to 25% gluten-free flours to a recipe without any noticeable change in the effect of the natural gluten.

If you have been using flour from the same bag for some months, you may notice that your loaves are gradually getting lower. One reason this may be happening is that the gluten is gradually dissipating from the flour. If this happens, it is possible to buy gluten, or gluten flour, separately to add to your bread mix.

---

tip

Gluten II *No rule of thumb tells you how much gluten to add, as you cannot measure the degree to which the natural gluten has dissipated. You could start off by adding 5 mL (1 tsp) of gluten and observing the result. If this is not enough, add 10 mL (2 tsp) to the next mix, then 15 mL (1 tsp). If the bread still does not rise, the problem is probably something else.*

The most commonly available and most commonly used flour for bread is made from hard wheat varieties. Grown mostly in Canada's Prairie provinces, this hard wheat is different from the wheat used for making cakes, pies and cookies. That is usually made from soft wheat or a mixture of hard and soft wheats.

Other flours, especially those labelled cake-and-pastry flour, are unsuitable for bread as they do not have sufficient gluten, which means the dough will not develop the elasticity desirable for bread. In a similar fashion, using bread flour for cakes and pastries will result in tough, chewy pastry.

Canada has won worldwide acclaim for its wheat, especially its hard wheat. For bread makers, the most important of these wheat strains came from Marquis wheat, first developed as a hybrid in 1903. The benefits of this wheat are that it matures earlier than most varieties, resists disease and has a high amount of naturally occurring gluten. It results in an excellent baking flour, which provides a consistently high elasticity in the dough.

If there is one important factor in consistently good bread baking, it is to ensure a consistently high quality of ingredients. At one time I had an unusually large number of requests for help from bread machine users in a Western Canada community. After some investigation I found that one of the home bakers had gone to the United States and bought inexpensive flour for all her friends. The flour was the common problem. I was able to help them by suggesting some recipe modifications, but the money they wasted by mixing good ingredients with cheap flour was certainly an example of false economy.

We are lucky that all-purpose white flour is standardized across Canada, with only very small variations from brand to brand. I do not recommend any specific brand here as they are all good. Most automatic bread machine recipe books recommend bread flour, primarily because they are written for the American market. Bread flour generally has not been available in Canadian stores, other than in specialty stores that cater to home bread bakers. Canadian all-purpose white flour has the same high gluten content found in bread flour sold in the United States and is an appropriate substitute.

Commercial bakeries are always able to have the right flour on hand, because they have a fast turnover of ingredients. Consistent quality is mandatory for continuing in business, so the baker orders special combinations and blends of flour to suit the specific product being made. These special flours may include a richer gluten content, more soft wheat or other specialty flours.

WHEAT FLOUR

All-purpose white

All-purpose white is the most highly refined flour that is commonly available. The major milling companies in Canada provide a consistently high quality of all-purpose white flour, which should give you consistent results in your bread machine.

All-purpose white flour is wheat flour that has had its wheat germ and bran removed during refining. The refining process also removes a number of natural nutrients in the flour, including the B vitamins, thiamin, niacin, riboflavin, vitamin E and iron. Current legislation compels flour companies to compensate for this loss by enriching the flour with thiamin, niacin, riboflavin and iron.

All-purpose white flour will retain its gluten content and therefore its bread making characteristics for up to a year or more. Even if your flour has lost its gluten content, there is no need to throw it away. It can be used in other recipes calling for flour.

I strongly recommend that you note the milling date (numbers and letters) of your flour, which is marked on every bag. This is a frustrating exercise, though, as it is very difficult to decipher milling code dates. With some diligent detective work you may pick up the pattern. If you transfer flour from the bag into another container, mark the container with the milling date. Do not mix flours with different milling dates in the same storage container. (You can, of course, mix flours in a recipe.) In many cases the independent millers in Western Canada produce a very high gluten-content flour and you may be able to check its milling date from the mill.

Whole wheat flour

Whole wheat flour contains the total grain, making it rich in fibre, nutrients and flavour. It can be made from any type of wheat, but if you're making bread, the whole wheat flour you use should be milled from hard wheat. The whole wheat flour on your supermarket shelves is not labelled as hard wheat, but it usually is, so it can be used in your automatic bread machine. If you buy your whole wheat flour from a specialty store, or the mill, be sure to request flour from hard wheat, or one suitable for yeast breads.

Within two to three months after milling, the fat in the wheat germ in whole wheat flour becomes rancid, the gluten dissipates and it is impossible to use the flour to make bread. When whole wheat flour was in regular use and people took their own wheat to be milled, they knew the exact milling date, and old flour was seldom a problem. When people started to buy whole wheat flour from the local store, before modern refrigeration, they did not know how well it had been kept and it was difficult for them and the store to keep the flour from becoming rancid during warm seasons. Nowadays, if you store your whole wheat flour in the refrigerator it will keep well.

I have not been able to find any evidence that rancid wheat germ does anything other than slightly affect the flavour of your baking, being unnoticeable in most cases. Older flour can still be used for muffins, quick breads and pancakes.

Graham flour

Graham flour was developed in the 1830s by evangelist-turned-food-reformer Sylvester Graham, who removed wheat germ and bran from whole wheat flour, then added back the bran. Since the wheat germ is the part of the grain that can become rancid, the result is a reasonably high-fibre flour that will stay fresh a few months longer than whole wheat.

Barley flour

Barley flour has been used in bread making in Canada since Canadians started making bread. There are three main reasons for its popularity. First, it was easily available as it has been a common crop in many parts of the country since the first immigrants came to Canada. Second, it improves the keeping quality of a bread. Third, it imparts a sweet flavour.

Even though barley is very low in gluten, it can be substituted for one-quarter of the wheat flour in bread made in an automatic bread machine. Whole barley flour, which includes the bran, is available in some areas and is a more nutritious choice. Both whole barley flour and barley flour mixed with wheat flours produce good quality bread.

Rye flour

Rye flour produces an interesting flavour long appreciated by Europeans, primarily because it was the only flour commonly available to them.

While rye flour contains some gluten, it is not enough to produce a satisfactory loaf in an automatic bread machine if used alone. For best results, rye flour should be used in combination with wheat flour so that the rye is only 25% of the total mix. Rye breads are traditionally low and heavy with a fine, dense texture.

Light rye flour is milled to exclude the bran, like all-purpose flour. Dark rye flour, sometimes called pumpernickel flour, contains bran and produces a rougher texture. You can use either type of rye flour in the recipes in this book with excellent results.

Some bread machine recipe books call for gluten to be added to every rye bread recipe. These recipes are not Canadian and do not take into account that our high-gluten wheat flours can support the rye in the loaf.

Storage
Use only fresh rye flour and store it in a cold place, like your freezer.

Triticale flour

This high-protein grain was developed by Canadian scientists to allow less fertile growing areas of the world to produce a grain that could provide nutritious flour.

Triticale is a hybrid of wheat and rye, with a nutty rye-like flavour. Like rye flour it does not have a high gluten content. It is not possible to substitute triticale flour for all the wheat flour in a recipe, but you can substitute up to half the amount. Triticale flour is always whole grain and therefore highly favoured by the health conscious.

Spelt flour

Usually ground as a whole grain flour, spelt has a nutty, sharp flavour when baked and is a favourite of people who follow holistic medical therapy. This ancient high-protein grain is from the same genus as wheat. It will grow in harsh conditions and was used extensively until about 200 years ago. Spelt is seeing a comeback because it is so easy to grow in harsh climates and sparse soils. It has an excellent nutrient content.

Spelt flour can be mixed with wheat flour. If you use it on its own, you will find that the loaf does not rise as high as loaves made with wheat flours, but it will still be very tasty.

Kamut flour

Made from another ancient grain, Kamut flour is a member of the wheat, triticale and einkorn family. It is not widely distributed, but is available in a number of specialty stores. There has been a revival of interest in the grain because of its high nutrient content and good flavour. Some people on restricted diets also find they are able to tolerate kamut flour better than other flours.

Kamut is similar to Durum – they are both excellent pasta flours – and has been used in the northern Mediterranean area since 4000 B.C.

FLOURS WITHOUT GLUTEN

Oat flour

Oat flour is made from the hulled oat kernel, which is milled into a fine flour. There is no gluten in oat flour. Therefore, when using it in yeast breads it is best to have oat flour as 25% or less of the flour in a recipe. Groats, which you may find in your bulk food store, are oat kernels before milling. Oat bran, which is the layer next to the hull of the kernel, is removed during the milling process. It is used in breads and cereals to add fibre to the diet. Rolled oats, sometimes called oatmeal, contain the entire edible part of the grain, minus the hull, and should not be used in the place of oat flour.

Corn flour

Generations of Canadian cooks have used coarsely ground corn or cornmeal to make sweet textured breads, muffins and quick breads. The cornmeal without the germ is ground into either white or yellow flour. Its addition to bread provides a pleasing flavour and gives a characteristic coarse texture to breads.

Corn starch is not used except in gluten-free breads. In some countries outside North America, corn starch is called corn flour.

Rice flour

Rice flour comes as brown rice flour and white rice flour. The difference is that brown rice flour includes the bran and therefore many of the nutrients naturally occurring in rice. The bran and many of the nutrients are removed in the refining process to make white rice flour. Sometimes a dusting of rice flour can be used for rolls and the like to make handling easier, but it is not a common ingredient in yeast doughs.

Bean flours

Bean flour is high-protein, high-fibre flour. Small amounts can be used in bread dough. Usually bean flour comes from soy beans, Romano beans or chick-peas.

Buckwheat flour

Buckwheat flour was a great favourite with the early Canadian settlers. Europeans grew buckwheat when they came to Canada because it could withstand the poor soil and harsh climate and had a short growing season. Small amounts of buckwheat flour or coarse groats from the buckwheat can add something special to both the flavour and texture of your bread.

tip

Flour

Special flours are available at bulk food and health food stores.

Quinoa

Made from a grain native to South America, quinoa (pronounced keen-wa) was first used by the Incas centuries ago and will grow where other grains will not. Quinoa flour is often found in flake cereals and is used by people who wish to avoid gluten. Quinoa offers a pleasant addition to baked goods including breads and can be found either as a flour or as a whole grain resembling rice.

STORING FLOUR

In baking breads, as in all other baking, the results are better if the ingredients are fresh. You can keep flour in its original package if you wish, but it is advisable to put it into a sealable plastic bag and keep it in a cool location, such as the refrigerator. This discourages weevils.

When you buy all-purpose flour in large quantities, keep out what you can use in a week or two, and store it in a plastic or glass container. Store the remaining flour in a cold place. With whole wheat flour, keep small quantities in the refrigerator and larger quantities in the freezer. It is difficult to predict how long whole wheat flour will retain its gluten, but storage in the freezer may extend its life by three to five months.

YEAST

The one ingredient in bread making that causes the most trouble and frustration is the yeast. Yeast is a living organism and it requires constant care.

While several types of yeast are available in Canada, only two are recommended for use in bread machines. Depending on which yeast your machine calls for, look for instant yeast or active dry yeast. Yeast manufacturers have done their best to confuse the issue by adding all sorts of special names to their brands. So you must read the small print on the yeast label. As each bread machine has been designed to use a specific type of yeast, be sure that you select the right one, or your bread will not rise properly.

Yeast is a single-celled living fungus that is dormant until you wake it up. The major difference between instant and active dry yeasts is the temperatures at which it wakes up. The yeast you use will be active between room temperature and 50°C (140°F).

Earlier types of yeast had to be dissolved in sugar and warm water in order to get started. Current yeasts do not need much sugar to be activated. The carbohydrate content of the flour is sufficient to feed the yeast in French and Italian breads.

Once fed and the appropriate warm liquid is added, yeast produces carbon dioxide and ethyl alcohol, which give bread its distinctive yeasty aroma. It is the carbon dioxide, generated by the yeast and sugar interacting, that causes the dough to rise, or leaven. The carbon dioxide is caught in the stretching dough, forming the tiny air pockets that give bread its cellular texture.

As the current generation of home bread makers, we are very fortunate to have instant and active dry yeast. Our forebears did not have this advantage. The original commercial yeast (called compressed, fresh or cake yeast) came in crumbly blocks resembling dry feta cheese and had a shelf life of about three weeks when stored in a cool place. While still available, it is not suitable for bread machines.

Before the 1970s the only other available yeast was dry yeast (not to be confused with active dry yeast). It had to be sprinkled onto a solution of sugar and water, then hand-mixed into the dough with the other ingredients. Developed in the 1940s, dry yeast is still used by cooks today for hand-made, traditional yeast recipes.

Instant Yeast

A relatively recent addition to your supermarket shelves, instant yeast is designed to be mixed with the dry ingredients in your bread machine and requires only a small amount of sugar to activate it. Instant yeast is pre-fermented and dried before being ground into fine particles. Compared with active dry yeast, instant yeast is ground more finely. The naming of new brands can cause confusion, so read the label carefully. Here is just one example of how confusing it can be. One company uses the term quick rise for their yeast, another calls theirs bread machine yeast. While both are instant yeasts and may be used in your machine, the bread machine yeast usually has a small amount of ascorbic acid added as an enhancer.

Another factor that adds to the confusion is that instant yeast is not called for in many conventional cookbooks, although it has been in common use in commercial bakeries for many years.

Since bread machines were developed as miniature replicas of bakeries, instant yeast was chosen for bread machines.

Instant yeast is the most forgiving strain of yeast, because even if it accidentally gets wet, it will usually still

tip

Sugar
Adding a small quantity of sugar may be useful even when using instant yeast for recipes such as French, Italian and Portuguese bread, which normally do not contain sugar.

function properly. If your automatic bread machine does not have a separate yeast dispenser, place the instant yeast on top of the dry ingredients.

The automatic bread machine will provide the heat to warm the liquids and activate the yeast as part of the mixing and pre-warming cycle of your bread machine.

Active dry yeast

Designed to be added to dry ingredients, this granular product was the first modern refined yeast. Active dry yeast is much easier to use than its predecessors and can also be used in traditional recipes. In these recipes, active dry yeast can be fermented in sugar and water as well as being added to dry ingredients.

> **tip**
>
> **Liquids**   *If the instructions that come with your automatic bread maker are not completely clear, you should always put the liquids in first, followed by the dry ingredients and finally the active dry yeast on the top.*

Bread machines using active dry yeast will often require that liquids be warmed. Use a thermometer to determine the correct temperature because if the liquids are too hot they will kill the yeast. If the liquids are too cold the yeast will not ferment and the dough will not rise.

> **tip**
>
> *I have found that in some recipes with some machines, instant yeast can be substituted for active dry, but never the other way around. You may want to experiment with your machine.*

Buying and storing yeast

A number of brands of yeast are available in Canada. They come in a variety of packages. Some brands and packages are available in

Yeast II *I have written the recipes for use with instant yeast. Should your machine specify active dry yeast, use the following chart for the equivalents.*

Active Dry	Instant
7 mL (1½ tsp)	5 mL (1 tsp)
10 mL (2 tsp)	7 mL (1½ tsp)
12 mL (2½ tsp)	10 mL (2 tsp)

some areas while others are not, but bearing in mind that you are looking past the brand name at the generic name, you will find instant or active dry yeast is available in all parts of the country. The best and most economical way to buy it is in large vacuum-packed containers. Repackage it into smaller airtight containers, such as glass jars. Store what you will use in a few weeks in the refrigerator and freeze the remainder. Make sure the jars are full since air encourages deterioration. Yeast that is frozen should keep for up to a year.

Test Yeast For Freshness *To test yeast for freshness: Put about 125 mL (½ cup) warm water in a small bowl. The water should be about 40°C (110°F). Check it either with a thermometer or by ensuring it does not feel too hot on the inside of your wrist. Dissolve 5 mL (1 tsp) sugar in the warm water and then sprinkle on 5 mL (1 tsp) yeast. If the yeast is still good it should start to foam and turn beige in about 5 minutes. If it does not foam, it is no longer useful, so discard it.*

The loss of power is gradual so the yeast may foam, but not as much as fresh yeast. As an extra check you might wish to compare the foaming of yeast you know is fresh with yeast that has been in storage.

Unopened cans and packages, kept in dry, cool, dark storage will also keep for up to a year. If you buy the small triple packs, refrigerate the open pack, folded over several times to seal out the air.

While you can buy a large supply of yeast from a bulk store and then store it yourself, I don't recommend buying unsealed yeast since it is difficult to know how fresh it is and how ideal the storage conditions at the store and in transit have been.

Yeast that is past its prime but still foams a little can still be used as long as you increase the amount you add to the recipe – up to double. This may make the bread taste yeasty, but at least you can use up your old stock when it is difficult to make a trip to the store.

Since yeast is a living organism, there is no firm rule about compensating for lack of freshness, but as you gain more experience with your machine and experiment a little, you will develop the knowledge necessary to make compensations.

SWEETENERS

Sugar

Sugar or a similar sweetener is necessary to feed the yeast in the bread making process, so don't leave it out even if you are dieting. You need only a very small amount of sugar, but it really improves the texture of the bread, ensuring a fine-grained crumb and uniform small cells throughout. Be careful not to add too much sugar, as this will result in some very large cells or monstrous holes here and there in the bread. Sugar also enhances the browning of the crust. Traditional French and Italian bread

tip

Brown Sugar
You can easily soften brown sugar by putting 125 mL (½ cup) in a covered microwaveable dish with a few drops of water on the inside of the lid. Heat on High power in your microwave for 20 to 30 seconds and the moisture will be absorbed.

require no sugar, or the small amount needed to activate the yeast.

In most cases, people with diabetes should be able to eat home-made bread if they weigh the amount they eat, using the amount in their dietary equivalents. They should, however, avoid sweet breads and check with their dietitian before planning any variation from their usual diet.

When the recipes in this book call for sugar, assume granulated white sugar. As only small quantities are needed, you will probably be successful substituting brown sugar, or even honey or molasses if you wish.

Brown sugar is really just refined white sugar with the molasses added back. The darker brown sugar has more flavour, which I prefer. The food value of brown sugar is about the same as white and can be substituted equally. Always pack brown sugar into the measuring spoon or cup. Avoid using hard brown sugar as it can scratch the nonstick finish in your bread pan.

Honey

Honey gives a distinctive flavour and adds to the colour of white bread. You may find that the unpasteurized version has a more pronounced flavour. If you decide to substitute honey for sugar in your recipe, you should use equivalent amounts for sweetening. Honey acts like a liquid though, so in order to compensate, reduce the liquid by half the volume of honey used.

> ## tip
>
> **Honey** *If your honey has crystallized, microwave it in the open jar on High power for 10 seconds. Be sure to remove the lid, or the pressure of heated air in the jar may cause it to explode. If the honey is still crystallized, continue heating it at 10-second intervals until it is liquid.*

tip

Molasses *Molasses is very sticky and difficult to get off the spoon. I have found that if you measure the oil or other shortening before measuring the molasses, then the molasses rolls off the spoon.*

Molasses

Molasses has a distinctive flavour, long enjoyed in breads such as rye and whole grain. Molasses also gives these breads their characteristic dark colour.

You need only a small amount to give the flavour and colour you want in your bread. Although molasses is a sugar, its acid component can interfere with the yeast's action, so follow the recipe amounts given and do not increase the quantity to intensify the flavour or the colour.

tip

Corn Syrup *Although corn syrup has the same sweetening ability as sugar or honey, I do not recommend using it in bread machine recipes because it is difficult to achieve the correct moisture balance in the dough.*

LIQUIDS

Liquids cause the starch granules in the flour to swell and become gelatinous, making the dough pliable as it is being kneaded. Dough that has the correct consistency should hold a smooth, rounded shape rather than flow, yet it should not be too stiff or crumbly. Sometimes it is not easy to achieve the correct moisture in bread dough, due to humidity changes. If it is very warm and humid, you may find that the flour and other ingredients absorb more moisture from the air than usual.

If you use flour that has been refrigerated and leave it open to the air on a warm humid day, you will probably find that it acts differently. This is because moisture has been absorbed from the air, making the last loaf moister or softer than the first.

There are many liquids that can be used in your bread recipes. Each of these different liquids will impart a special flavour. When deciding which liquid to use, consider the different ways in which certain liquids react with other ingredients. The addition of special liquids will change the flavour of the bread, but will change the texture to a much greater degree.

Usually, liquids should be added to the bread machine at room temperature, not ice cold or straight out of the refrigerator. There is one exception – if you don't like to leave milk out on the counter for very long, use it straight from the refrigerator as I have done without any problems.

Some brands of bread machine require you to warm the liquid. You should follow the manufacturer's instructions and warm liquids to the recommended temperature.

tip

Egg *Many of the recipes you are using call for an egg as part of the liquid. The average medium-sized egg is the equivalent of ¼ cup (50 mL). If you wish to measure the egg more precisely, put the other liquid ingredients into the measuring cup, then add the egg, still in its shell. When you have the right amount of liquid, remove the egg, warm the liquid and break the egg into the pan. (Before doing this be very careful to wash the shell well with soap and water because egg shells may carry salmonella – bacteria that causes food poisoning.)*

Juices

If you decide to add fruit or vegetable juices to your bread, note that the high acid content in juices can reduce the power of the gluten so that the bread will not rise well or hold its height. This could result in a loaf with the appearance of a collapsed mushroom. The way to counter this effect is to cut the amount of fruit or vegetable juice to about one-third of the total liquid measure and use water for the remaining amount.

Milk

Milk is the most popular liquid to use for bread. It improves bread texture, and its fat and protein content helps to produce uniform cells. Milk is important in most diets and can provide nutritional enrichment for children, fussy eaters and older adults. You can use any type of milk, but whole milk provides the most nutrients, including those minute quantities of foliates and copper mandatory for baby's health.

If you wish, you can further enrich the bread with protein by using both fresh milk and powdered skim milk. When trying to control fat intake, use 2%, 1% or skim, but not for children. When using powdered milk you can add the water separately, provided you add the quantity of powdered milk and water to total the amount of liquid the recipe calls for. Milk gives a softer crust than other liquids.

tip

Allergy
If you are allergic to milk, substitute water, rice milk or soy milk wherever your recipe calls for milk.

tip

Dry Milk *To make the equivalent of one cup of fresh or buttermilk from powder: Put 50 mL (¼ cup) powder into a measuring cup and stir in water until it reaches 250 mL (1 cup) in total.*

Buttermilk

Buttermilk produces an attractive crust and flavour. Unused fresh buttermilk can be frozen right in the container. If your buttermilk is in a carton, be sure to fold down the top of the milk carton, put the carton in a plastic bag and seal it.

If you use buttermilk only occasionally, the powdered variety is handy to have on hand and keeps well.

Water

Water is the second most common liquid ingredient in bread. It is always available and easy to use.

Beer

When using beer in bread recipes it is better fresh, but even if it is flat, it will still add to the flavour. Beer helps make a light bread, due to its own carbon dioxide and yeast, called brewer's yeast. Beer produces a particularly good and traditional flavour in rye bread.

Potato water

An excellent liquid to use in making bread, potato water provides a subtle flavour and improves keeping quality. You can make all the potato water you need by adding extra water to the peeled potatoes you are boiling for lunch or dinner.

If you do not use it right away, you can refrigerate potato water for about five days, or freeze it in measured amounts for future use.

> ## tip
>
> **Purees** *Fruit and vegetable purées such as mashed potatoes can be used instead of liquids to produce distinctive flavours or colours. If you do not wish to make your own purée, baby food is a good substitute.*

SHORTENING, FATS AND OILS

Shortening and oil are an important part of yeast breads in that they improve the kneading process by lubricating the gluten, which results in more tender bread. Very little fat is used in bread recipes and all fats, shortenings and oils are interchangeable, so if you use only one type of oil for your cooking, you can use it in your bread machine.

Fats, even in very small quantities, improve the keeping quality and increase the tenderness of bread. This is evident when milk or eggs are used, even though they contain only a little fat. French bread does not contain any fat; as a result it has a more open, coarse texture and tends to dry out quickly.

Oils

Oils are the most commonly used fat in bread machine recipes. They are the easiest to measure and may produce better results if solid shortening is giving you problems. There are a number of oils that are available in your supermarket today and they are all clearly marked as to their content. With so much emphasis on healthy eating these days, we all consider very carefully which oils we buy. Canola oil has been around for many years but is only now gaining in popularity since it is a monounsaturated fat. Canada is one of the world's largest growers of canola so if you use canola oil, it has probably been grown and processed right here in Canada. Soya oil has also been used in Canada for a long time and is often combined with other vegetable oils. Soya oil is another healthy choice. In testing these recipes I used mostly canola oil, using soya on a few occasions as a comparison. I found no difference between them.

Oil is also very convenient for coating the top of shaped yeast doughs since it is easy to brush on.

Shortening

Some people prefer shortening or solid vegetable oil to liquid oil. They can be substituted freely. I prefer to use solid shortening for greasing baking pans when baking hand-shaped buns and breads because it holds on to the sides of the pan without melting as the oven temperature rises.

Margarine is essentially a liquid oil that has been hydrogenated to become solid. We look at margarine as a substitute for butter, but as a substitute for oil, margarine can provide the flavour of butter without its cholesterol.

If you are concerned about the ingredients of shortenings, solid vegetable oils or margarine, read the ingredients list carefully. Many manufacturers are pleased to tell you that their margarine is made entirely from corn, canola or soya oil. Other labels may hedge and say that their product "may contain" various oils. The reason for this is that the market for oils is variable and at any given time one oil may be cheaper or more readily available than another. It does not matter to the manufacturer what proportions of different oils are included as long as the flavour and price are right. So if you want to be sure that your margarine consists only of canola oil, make sure that the package says so.

Butter and lard

In many people's view, there is no substitute for butter. Butter produces the best flavour and texture of all the fats. However, we do not always want to use butter because of the cost, our dietary restrictions and the strength of its flavour. Butter is only listed first in the recipes when the flavour or texture of the bread benefits from its presence. If you prefer, you can substitute another fat, but you may lose some of the flavour.

Lard, which is solid animal fat, can be used in any of these recipes, but because of its high cholesterol, very few home cooks and bakers use it these days.

SALT

Salt's main function is to provide flavour to the bread, so adjust the quantity to suit your own taste. Salt also controls the action of the yeast so it will not over-ferment. If you follow a salt-free diet, simply leave out the salt and enjoy wonderful fresh bread the same as everyone else. The only difference, other than the taste, is that salt-free bread will be more porous with larger cells, due to more fermentation by the yeast.

FLAVOURINGS: HERBS, SEEDS, NUTS AND SPICES

Fresh herbs are a wonderful way to add flavour to your bread. A few spoonfuls of fresh herbs from your garden will not alter how the recipe works, but will add special flavour and make the bread your own.

> ### tip
>
> **Herbs** *I have found that 50% whole wheat bread makes the best base for a herb-flavoured bread. I often use my own herb garden as inspiration. All the following herbs work well: basil, dill, mint, thyme, lemon balm, lemon verbena, hyssop, tarragon, chives, marjoram, oregano, rosemary, sage and savoury.*

Make sure you wash herb leaves well in lots of fresh water, remove leaves from stems, except for parsley where the flavour is greatest in the stem. Then chop or cut with scissors and add at the beginning of the bread cycle.

Dried herbs are called for in some of the recipes because I have found that they give better flavour than fresh. Do not substitute fresh for dried when the recipe specifies dried herbs. However, if fresh herbs are not available, you can substitute dried. When you substitute dried for fresh, use one-third to one-half of the amount called for.

Seeds and nuts can be added to bread to provide added flavour or texture. Most seeds and cereal groats (coarse grind) absorb moisture, therefore extra moisture has to be added to the recipe to accommodate them. The opposite is also true, so that if you reduce the amount of seeds and cereal in a recipe, you must also reduce the moisture. If your recipe calls for a specific amount of seeds or nuts and you decide to vary the recipe, be careful to compensate for the variation.

You can substitute ingredients to change flavour, or when you do not have the actual items called for in the recipe, as long as those ingredients have similar characteristics. For instance, you can substitute almonds for walnuts without having to worry about the moisture content. All that will happen is that the flavour will change. Cracked rye absorbs moisture while nuts do not, so if you are making this substitution you will have to adjust the moisture.

If you decide to enhance your baking with seeds when they are not included in the recipe add 5 mL (1 tsp) of water to compensate.

If the seeds or nuts are to be sprinkled on shaped rolls, loaves or other baked goods, no added moisture is required.

Millet

Millet is a small round seed that adds a crunchy texture to bread. Millet can be purchased as meal and tastes like and makes a suitable substitute for cornmeal. Millet is also ground as flour and is particularly useful as it is one of the least allergenic grains. High in iron and riboflavin, it is well worth adding to your diet.

Amaranth

Amaranth is also a small yellow seed that looks like millet, so keep the two labelled. Amaranth has a nuttier flavour than millet and provides complete protein, which is especially important for vegetarians.

Sorghum

Also like millet, sorghum is a popular staple grain in Africa.

Flax

Flax or linseed adds texture, flavour and nutrients.

Sesame & poppy seeds

Sesame seeds and poppy seeds also add distinctive flavour when included in breads or sprinkled on rolls. A number of traditional breads, such as poppy seed buns, include sesame and poppy seeds.

Sunflower seeds

Sunflower seeds are popular due in part to their distinctive flavour and crunch. It is best to use unsalted sunflower seeds when making bread, so that you don't end up with too much salt in the loaf.

Multi-grain cereals

Multi-grain cereals are often named according to how many grains have been mixed together to make them. They may be called five-grain, seven-grain or twelve-grain. Red River Cereal is one of my favourite multi-grain mixes. These cereals usually contain mixtures of some of the following: cracked wheat, cracked rye, cracked triti-cale, soya grits, barley grits, cornmeal, millet meal, sunflower seeds, flax seeds, Durum grits, rolled oats. You can add multi-grain cereals dry, without cooking.

Spices

Spices are usually plant seeds and when fresh are very flavourful. Specialty breads of different nationalities often have a characteristic flavour due to a spice that is traditional in that bread. If you substitute another spice, you may still have a good flavour but it will not resemble the original.

One of my favourite spices is cinnamon: it enhances the flavour of so many other ingredients from dried fruits to nuts and, best of all, it is readily available. Nutmeg and mace are also favourites of mine, as are cardamom, anise and freshly ground black pepper.

Chapter Three

The Mechanics of Making Bread

ABOUT ADDING THE INGREDIENTS

Liquids

These recipes do not include temperature of liquids; that depends on your bread machine. Many models suggest using room temperature liquids at 20°C (71°F). If you are unsure of the temperature required for liquids, have them at room temperature. Several automatic bread machines state they require hot liquid – often the ones that call for active dry yeast. If this is the case with your machine, heat the liquid in these recipes. The easiest way to heat the liquid is to place your measuring cup in the microwave oven on High power for 30 to 40 seconds for 250 mL (1 cup) and 60 to 70 seconds for 325 mL (1¼ cups). The liquid should feel hot to the touch, but it is more accurate and safer to use a thermometer. If the liquid is steaming, it is too hot.

Home bakers love to try different ways to improve their bread. Some experiment by warming the liquid even though their manual calls for room temperature liquid. Sometimes you get better results when you warm the liquids to about 33°C (115°F) – warm to the touch.

Other ingredients

Add the ingredients in the order given in the recipe so as to minimize the chance that you will forget an ingredient. If your machine has a yeast dispenser, then you do not need to worry, but if it hasn't, keep the yeast away from the salt and sugar until both have been distributed throughout the dough. Salt slows the rising of the dough and sugar feeds the yeast so it rises too fast.

When using the timer to delay the bread baking, take special care to have liquids at the bottom of the bread pan and flour on top, with the yeast sitting high and dry on top of it.

HOW DOES YOUR BREAD MACHINE WORK?

When you are preparing to make your loaf, whether it is your first or your 101st, be sure to double-check that all the parts of the bread machine are in position. Nothing is more upsetting than to discover after you added all your ingredients that you have forgotten the dough rod. This will leave a hole in the side of the pan and liquid will be quick to find an escape route. If this happens, don't panic; just lift out the pan and scrape the contents into a bowl using a spatula or your clean fingers. (Some machines have the hole in the bottom of the pan which has a rubber gasket. With these machines it is better to turn the entire unit upside down over a large bowl. This will be easier with someone helping, even if he or she is doubled up with laughter. You will need to clean the entire unit to ensure the gasket seals properly before inserting the blade and dough rod, and returning the ingredients to the pan.)

tip

Cleaning *To avoid forgetting to put all the parts back before baking a loaf, get in the habit of storing the unit clean, reassembled and ready to use.*

All automatic bread machines make some noise when they are mixing and kneading, so consider this normal. But there are two warning sounds you should be listening for with your machine, when it is working, which are an indication of possible trouble. The first is when you can hear the motor straining. This may mean that you have not added sufficient liquid. The second is a sloshing noise as the dough is being beaten in the pan. This means that you have put in too much liquid. Both situations can be remedied during the mixing cycle.

OPENING THE LID

If you are like me, you want to know what is going on inside that machine. Perhaps your loaves have not been coming out as well as they should and you want to see the dough ball, or you are just curious – and why not?

One thing to remember is that you should never open the top of your machine during the final hour of operation, which is when the heat is building up for the final rising and baking. If you open the top during this stage, heat will escape with the result that the dough will not become hot enough to rise sufficiently or cook through. You can open the lid during the early stages, if you do it carefully, in order to fix any problems.

You can open the lid on most bread machines for a quick look any time during the first hour, if it is for less than one minute. For example, if you have just started the machine and find that there is still one ingredient sitting in a measuring cup that you forgot to put in, you can simply open the top and add the missed ingredient.

You may wish to check the moistness of the dough ball. If you need to add more water, do not leave the lid up while you go to get it; close the lid and reopen it to add water.

CHECKING THE DOUGH BALL

The dough ball is formed about five minutes into the kneading cycle. It should hold its shape, being neither too soft nor too firm. If it is too soft, the ball will start to flow into the corners of the pan and not maintain its nice round shape. If the dough is too firm, you will probably hear the motor straining and the dough ball will not hold together and will look dry.

When checking the dough ball, be careful. On most units the mixing paddles do not stop when the lid is opened and it is dangerous to put a probe or your finger in to touch the top of the ball to test its firmness. You will be able to tell whether the dough ball is too soft or too firm by just looking at it.

If you find that the dough is too soft or too firm, even though you have measured very carefully and put in the right amounts in the right order, it may be that the flour has absorbed extra moisture from the air, or dried out due to atmospheric influences. In other words, you cannot anticipate this problem, although you can correct it during the mixing process. So bear this in mind if it is very dry or very moist where you live, or if you have your air conditioning or heating on.

If the dough is too firm, you need to add more liquid right away, before the kneading process is complete. Regardless of the liquid used in the recipe, you should add warm water, 1 tablespoon (15 mL) at a time. The water will be absorbed very easily and should be trickled in so that you do not overdo it and end up with a dough that is too soft.

If the dough is too soft, you need to add more flour. Carefully sprinkle the flour, 1 tablespoonful (15 mL) at a time, as deeply into the pan as you can so that it doesn't blow out and make a mess. The dough should start to lose its fluidity and form a soft ball.

CARE OF YOUR AUTOMATIC BREAD MACHINE

Your automatic bread machine is easy to keep clean and in good working order.

You should frequently wipe the outside surface with a clean wet cloth containing a little dishwashing detergent to remove grease and dirt. Wipe off suds with a clean wet cloth, then dry with a lint-free cloth to remove streaks and produce a shine.

It is important to keep the inside of your bread machine clean. Crumbs that wedge in the most obscure places can interfere with sensors and burn, like the crumbs in a toaster or toaster oven that isn't kept clean.

When you take out the pan, you can see that the interior of your bread maker is metal. I always use a little dishwashing detergent on a cloth to remove any greasy film that accumulates on the inside wall of the machine and wipe out the machine every time I use it. This prevents a build-up of grease, which could prevent the thermostat from obtaining accurate readings.

Don't forget to wipe the inside of the lid. If your machine has a removable lid, it makes it easier to clean, but do not immerse the lid in water or it may fill up with water and be difficult to get perfectly dry. You can use a soft brush to clear the vents and use vinegar to clean the viewing window.

If you have a baked-on spill, try repeatedly wiping it with a soapy wet cloth, coupled with strong rubbing. If that does not work, place some paper towels soaked in soapy water, but not dripping, against the baked-on bits, without letting water drip into the interior. Leave the paper for at least an hour, then try some more hard rubbing with a cloth. Repeat as needed.

It is not necessary or desirable to use fancy spray cleaners inside your bread machine. Not only are they not required, but they could clog or damage the machine.

If you need to take more extreme measures to get the inside of your machine clean, try green scrubbies or steel wool soap pads. Be careful not to damage any of the wires, buttons or other projections on the interior wall by scrubbing too energetically. If you damage the sensors or controls, you may void the manufacturer's warranty.

A better idea: if you spill simply splash something on the bread machine interior or even the exterior of the pan, wipe it off before you start the cycle. If you have started the machine, you can stop the unit, wipe it out and start the cycle again. The ingredients will be just fine if they have been sitting in the pan for less than one hour.

Don't put your automatic bread machine into water and don't put water into your automatic bread machine, because water could get into the power or electronic controls and cause a short circuit or malfunction. It will also void your warranty.

All the bread pans in the machines currently on the market are made of aluminum. The thicker pans are cast aluminum and the thinner ones are stamped aluminum. All pans are lined with a non-stick material like Teflon. If you look after the interior surface of the pan and do not scratch it with sharp implements or abrasive cleaners, it should give you many years of nonstick service.

To keep the inside of the pan clean, all you need to do is wash it with dishwashing detergent and water, then rinse it. If your bread pan has dough turning rods, use a soft brush to clean off any dough stuck in the little cracks in the rod or where it fits in the pan. Be careful to remove any hardened ingredients floating around in the pan – they could scratch the inside.

Always take the blade and rod out of the pan when you finish baking bread, otherwise you will find you have a little brown "washer" of baked-on dough that has formed under the kneading blade. If you don't remove the blade every time you use the machine, that dough washer can interfere with the functioning of the unit.

If you can't pull the kneading blade off the shaft easily, put some warm water in the pan and let it soak for about 10 minutes. The blade should then pull off easily.

Sometimes the kneading blade gets stuck in the bottom of the bread. I have found the easiest way to remove the blade is to use a wooden chopstick: the end is usually thin enough to insert into the hole in the blade and the stick provides good leverage for pulling the blade out.

Kneading blades and even dough rods may stay in the bread more often as your unit ages. I have found that if I spray the assembled interior of the bread pan with cooking spray, the bread comes out more easily, and the rod and paddle more often stay in the pan instead of coming out in the bread.

The exterior of the pan does not normally have a nonstick surface so it may start to develop a yellow film of grease. It can be cleaned with a green scrubby and dishwashing liquid.

Automatic bread machine manufacturers usually tell you not to put the pan in water at all. This is because some people will leave the pan soaking in soapy water for more than one minute, which removes some of the lubrication in the bearings in the bottom of the pan, with the result that they wear out more quickly. You can clean the exterior of the pan without submerging it in water; just rinse it under running water.

Chapter Four

Using This Book

SETTING THE SIZE

Some machines have been designed for two or more sizes of loaves. These sizes have been arbitrarily selected by the manufacturer. Some manufacturers talk about a regular loaf and a large loaf, others talk about a 1 lb loaf, a 1½ lb loaf and a 2 lb loaf, others have a small, medium and large loaf and others have regular, large and extra large. I have provided recipes for two sizes of loaf in this book. The only way to determine which recipe size your machine can handle is to look at the amount of flour that is called for in your manual's basic white bread recipe. If your manual calls for 500 mL (2 cups) of flour make the "small" recipe; if your manual calls for 750 mL (3 cups) of flour, make the "large" recipe. You can make the small-size loaves in a large-size machine if you like.

Once you have selected the size of recipe for your bread machine, highlight it in the book with a marker or ruler so you do not lose your place.

MEASURING INGREDIENTS PROPERLY

Many of the best cooks, my mother among them, measure their ingredients in whatever measuring cup is handy and then add a dash of this and a pinch of that. This is fine when you are cooking on top of a stove, in the oven or in a microwave, where you can watch, taste and adjust. With an automatic bread machine you have to change your approach to measuring ingredients because the amount of each ingredient plays an important part in not only the taste and texture of your bread, but also its chemistry.

When I was studying home economics at university we were very fussy. We had to take the flour that we were measuring and fluff it with a fork before putting it into the measuring cup. That way we got a consistent weight in each cup. We also calibrated our scales on a regular basis and tested all our measures against a standard measure.

This complicated approach is not practical for people cooking in their own kitchens, the recipe testers and I tested these recipes in our home kitchens, with all the variations in humidity and temperature that you will get in your own home.

We did, however, use standard measuring techniques and proper measuring tools. They are not expensive and I recommend that in order to get good, consistent results you follow a few simple rules of measuring and use the proper measures.

I have found liquid measuring cups, with a pouring spout, in three useful sizes: 250 mL (one cup), 500 mL (two cup), and 1000 mL (four cup). These cups have metric and imperial measures on them. Plastic and glass cups work equally well. However, not all measuring cups are entirely accurate. I have found that the two glass companies – Pyrex and Anchor Hocking – have accurate measures.

Dry ingredients should be measured in nesting cups that each have a specific volume so that you can level off the ingredient with the straight edge of a metal spatula, ruler or handle of a rubber spatula. You cannot accurately level off flour in a liquid measuring cup.

When you are looking for nesting dry measures, do not buy those with both metric and imperial measures on them. A measure of 250 mL is not equal to one 8 oz cup. They are both precise measures but are not interchangeable. I have found that the name brand cups such as Rubbermaid and Tupperware are accurate.

Whichever system you decide to use, be consistent and do not switch between imperial and metric columns in recipes. Inconsitent conversions are the main problem with recipes in most other cookbooks.

I have found my recipes work best using the metric system. If you do not want to get new measures at this time, add them to your Christmas or birthday wish list. In the meantime, monitor your dough so you have an indicator of the accuracy of your measures and/or your technique.

If you are buying metric cups, you need 50 mL, 125 mL and 250 mL measures and 1, 2, 5, 15 and 25 mL spoons.

If you are buying imperial nesting cups, you will need measures for ¼, ⅓, ½ and 1 cup and ⅛, ¼, ½ and 1 teaspoon and 1 tablespoon. Some sets do not include the ⅛ teaspoon so you may have to find that elsewhere, or use half the ¼ teaspoon. Some sets include a 2 tablespoon measure, but it is not really necessary.

The two metric and imperial measures that are equivalents are 5 mL equals 1 teaspoon and 15 mL equals 1 tablespoon.

When measuring flour, mix the flour around in the bag or container with the measuring cup or spoon, then dip the cup down into the container, overfill it and level off the top by scraping the straight edge across it. This will give you a little heavier flour than measuring in the more conventional manner, but it is the easiest and is consistent with the manner in which I developed the recipes. Do not tap, pack or bump the cup before levelling or you will have even more in your measure than you should – up to 25% more.

tip

Measuring I *With soft fine ingredients, such as flour, always dip the measure into the bag or container until you get right down to the bottom. For granular dry ingredients such as Durum semolina and sugar, either dip your measure into the container or pour the ingredient into the measure.*

tip

Volume/Weight Equivalents

all-purpose flour	250 mL = 145 g	1 cup = 140 g
whole wheat flour	250 mL = 135 g	1 cup = 130 g

Measuring the flour, which is the largest single dry ingredient, is the most important step in bread making. The other ingredients used in most bread recipes are not as difficult to measure, or so little of them is used that precise measurement is less critical.

DEDICATED BREAD CYCLES

The early bread machines still make excellent bread, even though they may have only one baking and one dough cycle, since they were developed and manufactured in Asia, where basic white bread is preferred.

North American consumers demanded bread machine recipes for whole grain breads, sweet breads and European-style breads.

As manufacturers recognized that some flours need longer kneading, rising, or in the case of European flours, longer warming and soaking cycles, the original machines were updated to provide a variety of cycles.

All machines have a basic or white cycle, which is the one you will probably use most often. This is also the cycle you should use when no specific one is recommended. If the recipe you are using calls for more than 60% whole wheat flour, use the wheat or whole wheat cycle if you have one on your machine. If you don't, use the basic cycle: I have adapted the recipes in this book by substituting sufficient all-purpose flour, so the whole wheat recipes work with the basic cycle.

If you have a French Bread cycle on your machine, you can also use this same cycle for sourdough breads.

WHAT IS A PERFECT LOAF?

A perfect loaf is one that has risen to about twice the height of the raw ingredients when you put them in the pan. The outside should be evenly golden brown. The crust should be rounded and may have a stretched or split layer across the top, although photographs of loaves of bread rarely show this because it doesn't photograph well. There should not be flour on the outside of the loaf. A small recipe in a very large pan may not be as brown on top as a larger loaf.

Inside, the loaf should have uniform cells from top to bottom. These cells may be stretched either vertically or horizontally. Usually cells are not larger than the diameter of a pencil. When the cells are even, the bread is usually tender, so after a slice is squeezed it will spring back to its original shape.

IN SEARCH OF EXCELLENT BREAD

If you have a problem loaf, take a good look at a slice and you can probably find out what went wrong and correct it for the next loaf.

My loaf did not rise as high as usual. What went wrong?

First you need a benchmark against which to measure your loaf. I always use the "white" or basic loaf recipe as my benchmark. Whole wheat and many other breads will not rise as much as the "basic" or "white" bread.

❖ Remember that you may not put exactly the same amount of ingredients in each time, that the ingredients "age" at different speeds and the heat and humidity in your kitchen may be different at the times when you make the same loaves.

❖ If the bread is no higher than the ingredients were when you put them in, then your problem is probably the yeast. Test your yeast for freshness (see page 17) and throw it away if it doesn't pass.

❖ If the bread has risen, but is only about half-way up the pan, then the problem is probably the yeast again. First, check that you are using the right yeast. If you are sure it is the right yeast then test it. The yeast may be old, but if it is just "weak" it can still be used if you increase the amount, up to double, in the next loaf. The extra yeast will produce a more yeasty flavour in the bread.

❖ If the bread contains grains and flours other than all-purpose flour, the loaf may just come to the top of the pan, which is normal.

❖ If the bread is made of whole wheat flour, then it will not rise as much as white or basic bread. If it is not as high as your previous loaves made with the same recipe, the problem may be the age of the whole wheat flour. If you regularly bake whole wheat bread, after a while you will notice that each loaf rises a little less than its predecessor. This is caused by a gradual weakening of the gluten in the flour. To counter this, you can either substitute all-purpose white flour for up to 75% of the whole wheat flour or add 5 mL (1 tsp) of gluten per 250 mL (one cup) of flour.

❖ If the yeast and the whole wheat flour are both problem-free, check the temperature of the liquid you used. Was it too hot or too cold? Liquid that is too hot above 55°C (130°F) can destroy the yeast and liquid that is too cold will not bring it to life. For units that do not specify the temperature, room temperature is best.

The last bread I baked was dense, compact and low. What should I do?

First of all, don't throw it out: this bread will be just fine sliced very thin for open-faced sandwiches or toasted and spread with honey.

❖ The most common reason for dense bread is not enough liquid.

❖ A heavy loaf can also be caused by using old flour. Has it been stored properly in a cool, dark, airtight container? If not, this could accelerate the aging, especially in whole wheat flours.

❖ Too much salt will also cause a dense, compact, low loaf, because it will stop the yeast from doing its job.

❖ Loaves with vegetables or fruit may also be dense due to the moisture content of the ingredients. Next time you make this recipe, check the dough ball (see page 31) and make the necessary adjustments.

Why did my bread overflow the pan?

Some bread may rise so much that it flows out of the pan and over the sides leaving a big mess to clean up. Other times the bread may rise just a little too much so that it reaches the lid and burns a little on the lid.

- ❖ If the loaf has risen very high and contains very large air-spaces at the top, you probably added too much yeast. Sometimes the loaf will rise so high that it collapses, resulting in a flat loaf – a different result but the same cause.

- ❖ Another cause of over-rising is too much sugar, which over-activated the yeast. You can tell that the trouble is the sugar if you see too much browning on top of the loaf, caused by burned sugar.

- ❖ If the loaf has too much liquid, the cell walls will be too thin to hold up and will collapse. This may mean you put too much liquid in the recipe, or it may mean the weather was very humid, which often has the same effect. If the weather is just as humid when you bake the next loaf, reduce the liquid or add up to 50 mL (¼ cup) flour to the dough ball, a spoonful at a time.

- ❖ If you adapted the recipe by adding an egg where the recipe does not call for one, you may have failed to compensate for the extra liquid of the egg.

- ❖ This may have happened because you live at a very high altitude. Reduce the yeast by one-quarter and the liquid by 15 mL (1 tbsp).

My last loaf rose so high I had to scrape the top crust off the inside lid. It tasted great, but it made a mess I don't want to repeat.

- ❖ The most common cause is too much liquid. If you have been adapting a recipe, make sure your measures are correct. Check the dough ball before kneading.

❖ Another common cause is too much sugar, which increases yeast's activation; raisins and other dried fruit also contain a great deal of sugar and may contribute to over-rising.

❖ Adding eggs to a recipe that does not have eggs without adjusting the liquids to compensate for the liquid in the egg could also result in over-rising.

Why didn't my bread rise as much as it did previously?

❖ This usually occurs when yeast is aging. Just add a little extra yeast next time. Test yeast to check how potent your yeast still is. Buy new yeast so you are not caught without good yeast.

❖ If this happened when whole wheat flour was used, then you can be sure that the whole wheat flour is getting old. Check the information in Chapter 2 to determine what course to follow.

What causes large coarse cells in my bread?

❖ Usually there is a combination of problems. For example, the atmosphere may be very humid and the electrical power a bit lower than usual because of the air conditioner cycling on and off.

❖ Too much salt or substituting too much water for milk can also cause a coarser loaf.

Why is my bread paler in colour than usual?

❖ If you have started to cut back on sugar, it will reduce the browning of the crust. Increasing sugar will restore the browning.

❖ The problem may be electrical: the voltage in your kitchen may have dropped for some reason. If you know there is a temporary power brown-out problem, increase the top browning setting until the power returns to normal.

❖ If there is a viewing window on your bread machine, then the glass may be preventing the heat from being reflected back onto the baking loaf and browning it. If you want a darker loaf, set the browning control to maximum. If that doesn't work, cover the glass on the inside of the lid with aluminum foil. If necessary, use aluminum tape to hold it in place. Remember to keep the foil curved against the top but away from vents.

Why is my loaf darker than usual?

❖ This usually means too much sugar, whether due to inaccurate measurement, adding more sugar than the recipe called for or adding dried fruits such as raisins or dried apricots. To correct, select a setting that gives you a lighter crust.

What causes that unattractive ropy top crust I sometimes get?

❖ You probably have too much flour or not enough liquid. If the recipe worked well on previous occasions, was your kitchen temperature or humidity different? When making your next loaf, check the dough at the kneading stage to see if there is sufficient liquid. If necessary, add warm water a spoonful at a time. Keep track of the amount added as it may be necessary to do this each time the humidity drops.

Generally poor results when making bread in your automatic bread baker might be caused by the environment. When you turn air conditioning on or off for the season, or if the weather is very changeable, you will find that the small sensors in your bread machine take a few days to acclimatize. Your bread might reflect this change in the environment, by either over-rising or being too dense for a few days, until the sensors adjust to the new environment.

Chapter Five

Loaves

*T*he recipes in this book were written to work in all bread machines in Canada. Please note:

❖ If the recipe calls for water and the instruction manual for your bread machines tells you to use "hot tap water" then do so, because unlike some machines your machine obviously does not heat the water as part of its program.

❖ When the recipe calls for yeast, if your machine requires "instant" yeast use "instant" yeast, if the book for your machine calls for "active dry" yeast then use "active dry" yeast. All recipes have been tested with the appropriate yeast called for by the manufacturer. If the manual on your machine does not specify which yeast to use or is unclear, use instant.

---

tip

High Altitude *People hear that high altitude affects baking, but that usually concerns fragile batters like cakes and muffins. Breads are not usually affected by high altitude. Still, it is possible, so here's what to look for, and what to do. First, check all the ingredients to be sure that the correct amounts were put in and that the ingredients are fresh. It is best to make another loaf. If you are sure that you didn't make any mistakes in the recipe, try reducing the yeast or sugar by half. Keep a record of your changes so you can make the corrections if you need to in future.*

VARIATIONS ON WHITE

Basic White Loaf

A simple homemade white has flavour and texture that is missing in most store-bought loaves.

	Small Loaf		Large Loaf	
	Metric	**Imperial**	**Metric**	**Imperial**
All-purpose flour	500 mL	2 cups	750 mL	3 cups
Salt	5 mL	1 tsp	7 mL	1½ tsp
Sugar	15 mL	1 tbsp	25 mL	2 tbsp
Oil	15 mL	1 tbsp	25 mL	2 tbsp
Water or milk	225 mL	⅞ cup	350 mL	1⅓ cups
Yeast	5 mL	1 tsp	7 mL	1½ tsp

> **tip**
>
> **Testing**   *Also, use this Basic White Loaf for testing the freshness of your ingredients or testing the function of your bread machine.*

Barley Loaf

Barley gives a more defined flavour, which I love. It has been used in bread since the first settlers came to Canada.

	Small Loaf		Large Loaf	
Barley flour	125 mL	½ cup	250 mL	1 cup
All-purpose flour	375 mL	1½ cups	500 mL	2 cups
Salt	5 mL	1 tsp	7 mL	1½ tsp
Sugar	15 mL	1 tbsp	25 mL	2 tbsp
Oil	15 mL	1 tbsp	25 mL	2 tbsp
Potato water	225 mL	⅞ cup	325 mL	1¼ cups
Yeast	5 mL	1 tsp	7 mL	1½ tsp

French Loaf

To keep the crusty surface on this loaf, store it in a paper bag.

	Small Loaf		Large Loaf	
Durum semolina flour	125 mL	1½ cups	250 mL	1 cup
All-purpose flour	350 mL	1½ cups	500 mL	2 cups
Salt	5 mL	1 tsp	7 mL	1½ tsp
Water	250 mL	1 cup	325 mL	1⅓ cups
Yeast	7 mL	1½ tsp	10 mL	2 tsp

tip

Yeast III   *Open a can of yeast with a can opener instead of a punch. This way you can dip your spoon in to measure and level it off, letting the extra spill back into the can.*

Portuguese Corn Loaf

With the similar texture of French bread, this popular loaf has corn flour as the secret to its particular flavour.

	Small Loaf		Large Loaf	
Corn flour (white or yellow)	125 mL	½ cup	200 mL	¾ cup
All-purpose flour	375 mL	1½ cups	625 mL	2⅓ cups
Salt	5 mL	1 tsp	7 mL	1½ tsp
Oil	10 mL	2 tsp	15 mL	1 tbsp
Water	225 mL	⅞ cup	325 mL	1⅓ cups
Yeast	7 mL	1½ tsp	10 mL	2 tsp

Lemony Potato Loaf

A hint of garlic and onion contribute zest to this heavy-textured, filling bread.

	Small Loaf		*Large Loaf*	
All-purpose flour	250 mL	1 cup	375 mL	1½ cups
Whole wheat flour	250 mL	1 cup	375 mL	1½ cups
Mashed potatoes*	125 mL	½ cup	200 mL	¾ cup
Garlic powder	0.5 mL	⅛ tsp	1 mL	¼ tsp
Dry mustard	0.5 mL	⅛ tsp	1 mL	¼ tsp
Salt	5 mL	1 tsp	7 mL	1½ tsp
Sugar	5 mL	1 tsp	7 mL	1½ tsp
Grated lemon peel	5 mL	1 tsp	10 mL	2 tsp
Lemon juice	5 mL	1 tsp	10 mL	2 tsp
Olive oil	15 mL	1 tbsp	25 mL	2 tbsp
Chopped onion	25 mL	2 tbsp	50 mL	¼ cup
Potato water or water	175 mL	⅔ cup	250 mL	1 cup
Yeast	5 mL	1 tsp	7 mL	1½ tsp

*If using instant mashed potato flakes	75 mL	1/3 cup	125 mL	½ cup

Romano Bean Loaf

Romano or whole bean flour, available at bulk food stores, adds protein and an interesting, mild flavour.

	Small Loaf		Large Loaf	
All-purpose flour	425 mL	1⅔ cups	625 mL	2½ cups
Romano bean flour	75 mL	⅓ cup	125 mL	½ cup
Salt	5 mL	1 tsp	7 mL	1½ tsp
Sugar	15 mL	1 tbsp	25 mL	2 tbsp
Oil	15 mL	1 tbsp	25 mL	2 tbsp
Water	250 mL	1 cup	350 mL	1⅓ cups
Yeast	5 mL	1 tsp	7 mL	1½ tsp

Wild Rice Loaf

A friend's father inspired this loaf with his version. It is very like French bread in texture and makes a good sandwich.

	Small Loaf		Large Loaf	
Cooked wild rice	75 mL	⅓ cup	125 mL	½ cup
Rice flour	125 mL	½ cup	200 mL	¾ cup
All-purpose flour	375 mL	1½ cups	550 mL	2¼ cups
Thyme	1 mL	¼ tsp	2 mL	½ tsp
Salt	7 mL	1½ tsp	10 mL	2 tsp
Sugar	15 mL	1 tbsp	25 mL	2 tbsp
Margarine	15 mL	1 tbsp	25 mL	2 tbsp
Water	225 mL	⅞ cup	325 mL	1¼ cups
Yeast	5 mL	1 tsp	7 mL	1½ tsp

tip

Wild Rice *To get the correct amount of wild rice, which expands to three times its volume when cooked, begin with 25 mL (2 tbsp) raw rice for a small loaf, 35 mL (3 tbsp) for a large one.*

Anise Seed Bread

During baking, you will notice the aroma of licorice; the flavour is more subtle.

	Small Loaf		Large Loaf	
All-purpose flour	500 mL	2 cups	750 mL	3 cups
Anise seeds	5 mL	1 tsp	7 mL	1½ tsp
Salt	5 mL	1 tsp	7 mL	1½ tsp
Sugar	25 mL	2 tbsp	35 mL	3 tbsp
Butter or margarine	25 mL	2 tbsp	35 mL	3 tbsp
Egg plus	1	1	2	2
Milk to equal	225 mL	⅞ cup	350 mL	1¼ cups
Yeast	5 mL	1 tsp	7 mL	1½ tsp

Corn and Potato Loaf

Make a whole meal of this by adding a meat filling for a sandwich.

	Small Loaf		Large Loaf	
All-purpose flour	500 mL	2 cups	750 mL	3 cups
Mashed potatoes*	125 mL	½ cup	200 mL	¾ cup
Corn kernels	125 mL	½ cup	200 mL	¾ cup
Finely chopped onion	25 mL	2 tbsp	35 mL	3 tbsp
Thyme	0.5 mL	⅛ tsp	1 mL	¼ tsp
Pepper	0.5 mL	⅛ tsp	1 mL	¼ tsp
Salt	5 mL	1 tsp	7 mL	1½ tsp
Butter or margarine	15 mL	1 tbsp	25 mL	2 tbsp
Milk	200 mL	¾ cup	250 mL	1 cup
Yeast	5 mL	1 tsp	7 mL	1½ tsp
*If using instant mashed potato flakes	75 mL	⅓ cup	125 mL	½ cup

tip

Flour III   *If you have ample freezer space and want to save money, buy large bags of flour when they are on sale. Rebag them in resealable plastic bags, date and store all but the one you are currently using in the freezer.*

Onion Lover's Loaf

Frying the onions first is the secret to this truly delicious onion bread.

	Small Loaf		Large Loaf	
All-purpose flour	500 mL	2 cups	750 mL	3 cups
Garlic powder	dash	dash	dash	dash
Black pepper	dash	dash	dash	dash
Poppy seeds	5 mL	1 tsp	7 mL	1½ tsp
Salt	5 mL	1 tsp	7 mL	1½ tsp
Sugar	10 mL	2 tsp	15 mL	1 tbsp
Water or milk	225 mL	⅞ cup	325 mL	1⅓ cups
Yeast	5 mL	1 tsp	7 mL	1½ tsp

In a small skillet fry the following mixture until the onions are tender, then add to ingredients in the bread pan:

Chopped onion	50 mL	¼ cup	75 mL	⅓ cup
Margarine or butter	10 mL	2 tsp	15 mL	1 tbsp

Ham and Pineapple Loaf

Easter dinner inspired this bread with its hint of cloves.

	Small Loaf		Large Loaf	
All-purpose flour	500 mL	2 cups	750 mL	3 cups
Crushed pineapple	125 mL	½ cup	200 mL	¾ cup
Chopped ham	50 mL	¼ cup	75 mL	⅓ cup
Salt	5 mL	1 tsp	7 mL	1½ tsp
Ground cloves	0.5 mL	⅛ tsp	1 mL	¼ tsp
Oil	5 mL	1 tsp	10 mL	2 tsp
Water	125 mL	½ cup	200 mL	¾ cup
Yeast	5 mL	1 tsp	10 mL	2 tsp

AROMATIC LOAVES

Herb and vegetable breads are not only for the adventurous bread maker. You might begin by buying your herbs and then later on growing and drying your favourites. Create your own mixtures for a unique loaf.

Aromatic Rosemary Loaf

The aroma of rosemary is highlighted during baking. However, the texture is like a white loaf.

	Small Loaf		Large Loaf	
All-purpose flour	250 mL	1 cup	375 mL	1⅔ cups
Whole wheat flour	175 mL	⅔ cup	250 mL	1 cup
Barley flour	50 mL	¼ cup	75 mL	⅓ cup
Salt	5 mL	1 tsp	7 mL	1½ tsp
Rosemary	1 mL	¼ tsp	2 mL	½ tsp
Sugar	15 mL	1 tbsp	25 mL	2 tbsp
Olive oil	15 mL	1 tbsp	25 mL	2 tbsp
Water	200 mL	¾ cup	300 mL	1¼ cups
Yeast	5 mL	1 tsp	7 mL	1½ tsp

Basil Cheese Loaf

You'll love the double cheese flavour teamed with basil.

	Small Loaf		Large Loaf	
Barley flour	75 mL	⅓ cup	125 mL	½ cup
All-purpose flour	425 mL	1¾ cup	625 mL	2½ cups
Black pepper	0.5 mL	⅛ tsp	1 mL	¼ tsp
Dried basil	2 mL	½ tsp	5 mL	1 tsp
Salt	2 mL	½ tsp	5 mL	1 tsp
Sugar	5 mL	1 tsp	7 mL	1½ tsp
Olive oil	15 mL	1 tbsp	25 mL	2 tbsp
Grated parmesan cheese	50 mL	¼ cup	75 mL	⅓ cup
Ricotta cheese(10% BF)	125 mL	½ cup	250 mL	1 cup
Water	125 mL	½ cup	175 mL	⅔ cup
Yeast	5 mL	1 tsp	7 mL	1½ tsp

Ricotta Dill Loaf

In the spring when fresh dill is coming up in the garden, add extra if you wish.

	Small Loaf		Large Loaf	
All-purpose flour	500 mL	2 cups	750 mL	3 cups
Pepper	0.5 mL	⅛ tsp	1 mL	¼ tsp
Salt	5 mL	1 tsp	7 mL	1½ tsp
Sugar	15 mL	1 tbsp	25 mL	2 tbsp
Oil	15 mL	1 tbsp	25 mL	2 tbsp
Snipped fresh dill	25 mL	2 tbsp	35 mL	3 tbsp
Ricotta cheese (10% BF)	125 mL	½ cup	175 mL	⅔ cup
Water	125 mL	½ cup	250 mL	1 cup
Yeast	5 mL	1 tsp	7 mL	1½ tsp

tip

Size II   *You can make a small loaf in a machine that says it will make large loaves, without a problem. Use the small recipe in this book. You should get a lovely loaf half the height and size of the larger loaf.*

Garden Loaf

My vegetarian neighbours love the flavour of this bread, which complements their diet.

	Small Loaf		Large Loaf	
All-purpose flour	250 mL	1 cup	375 mL	1½ cups
Whole wheat flour	250 mL	1 cup	375 mL	1½ cups
Black pepper	dash	dash	dash	dash
Garlic powder	dash	dash	dash	dash
Sugar	10 mL	2 tsp	15 mL	1 tbsp
Vegetable soup powder	10 mL	2 tsp	15 mL	1 tbsp
Fresh mint	25 mL	2 tbsp	35 mL	3 tbsp
Oil	15 mL	1 tbsp	25 mL	2 tbsp
Grated carrot	100 mL	⅓ cup	125 mL	½ cup
Water	225 mL	⅞ cup	300 mL	1¼ cups
Yeast	5 mL	1 tsp	7 mL	1½ tsp

Vegetable Loaf

This moist loaf with almost all the garden included makes delicious sandwiches.

	Small Loaf		Large Loaf	
All-purpose flour	375 mL	1⅓ cups	550 mL	2¼ cups
Whole wheat flour	75 mL	½ cup	175 mL	⅔ cup
Wheat bran	50 mL	¼ cup	75 mL	⅓ cup
Thyme	0.5 mL	⅛ tsp	1 mL	¼ tsp
Pepper	0.5 mL	⅛ tsp	1 mL	¼ tsp
Salt	5 mL	1 tsp	7 mL	1½ tsp
Oil	15 mL	1 tbsp	25 mL	2 tbsp
Grated zucchini	200 mL	¾ cup	250 mL	1 cup
Chopped onion	15 mL	1 tbsp	25 mL	2 tbsp
Chopped green pepper	15 mL	1 tbsp	25 mL	2 tbsp
Chopped mushrooms	75 mL	⅓ cup	125 mL	½ cup
Water	125 mL	½ cup	225 mL	¾ cup
Yeast	5 mL	1 tsp	7 mL	1½ tsp

tip

Vegetables   *Vegetables make great flavour; however, they carry a great deal of moisture. Measure carefully and check the dough during the first kneading to make sure it is not too soft. Add extra flour if needed (see p. 31).*

Mediterranean Loaf

The inspiration comes from eating olives and bread with oil. Here they are all together.

	Small Loaf		Large Loaf	
All-purpose flour	250 mL	1 cup	375 mL	1½ cups
Whole wheat flour	250 mL	1 cup	375 mL	1½ cups
Oregano	1 mL	¼ tsp	2 mL	½ tsp
Thyme	1 mL	¼ tsp	2 mL	½ tsp
Grated lemon peel	2 mL	½ tsp	5 mL	1 tsp
Salt	5 mL	1 tsp	7 mL	1½ tsp
Sugar	15 mL	1 tbsp	25 mL	2 tbsp
Olive oil	15 mL	1 tbsp	25 mL	2 tbsp
Chopped ripe olives	35 mL	3 tbsp	50 mL	¼ cup
Water	200 mL	¾ cup	300 mL	1¼ cups
Yeast	5 mL	1 tsp	7 mL	1½ tsp

Onion Cheddar Loaf

Everyone loves cheese bread, but use only as much cheese as indicated. Remember, old Cheddar has the most flavour.

	Small Loaf		Large Loaf	
All-purpose flour	250 mL	1 cup	375 mL	1½ cups
Whole wheat flour	250 mL	1 cup	375 mL	1½ cups
Chopped onion	50 mL	¼ cup	75 mL	⅓ cup
Cubed cheddar cheese*	50 mL	¼ cup	75 mL	⅓ cup
Pepper	0.5 mL	⅛ tsp	1 mL	¼ tsp
Tarragon or savory	1 mL	¼ tsp	2 mL	½ tsp
Salt	5 mL	1 tsp	7 mL	1½ tsp
Sugar	5 mL	1 tsp	10 mL	2 tsp
Oil	5 mL	1 tsp	10 mL	2 tsp
Water	200 mL	¾ cup	300 mL	1⅓ cups
Yeast	5 mL	1 tsp	7 mL	1½ tsp

*Cheese can be coarsely grated but you will get better flavour if you cut it in 5 mm (¼") cubes.

Tabbouleh Loaf

Middle-Eastern flavours with just a hint of mint and onion combine to appeal to the palate. Make the bulgur first.

	Small Loaf		Large Loaf	
Water	50 mL	¼ cup	75 mL	⅓ cup
Bulgur (or cracked wheat or cracked rye)	50 mL	¼ cup	75 mL	⅓ cup

In a cup, pour water over bulgur and set aside for 15 minutes then add to flour mixture in bread pan.

	Small Loaf		Large Loaf	
Whole wheat flour	125 mL	½ cup	250 mL	1 cup
All-purpose flour	375 mL	1½ cups	500 mL	2 cups
Black pepper	0.5 mL	⅛ tsp	0.5 mL	⅛ tsp
Salt	5 mL	1 tsp	7 mL	1½ tsp
Sugar	5 mL	1 tsp	7 mL	1½ tsp
Lemon juice	5 mL	1 tsp	10 mL	2 tsp
Olive oil	15 mL	1 tbsp	25 mL	2 tbsp
Dried mint	7 mL	1½ tsp	15 mL	1 tbsp
Chopped green onion	1	1	2	2
Tomato, seeded and chopped plus Water to equal	100 mL	½ cup	250 mL	1 cup
Yeast	5 mL	1 tsp	7 mL	1½ tsp

GOODNESS GRAINS

One way to add interesting flavour and aroma to your bread is to use different grains. Don't be afraid to experiment with them.

Canadian Grain Loaf

This loaf includes grains commonly grown in most of the country, with the additional crunch of unsalted sunflower seeds.

	Small Loaf		Large Loaf	
Cornmeal	50 mL	¼ cup	75 mL	⅓ cup
Barley flour	50 mL	¼ cup	75 mL	⅓ cup
Rye flour	50 mL	¼ cup	75 mL	⅓ cup
Rolled oats	50 mL	¼ cup	75 mL	⅓ cup
Graham flour	125 mL	½ cup	200 mL	¾ cup
All-purpose flour	250 mL	1 cup	375 mL	1½ cups
Sunflower seeds	50 mL	¼ cup	75 mL	⅓ cup
Salt	5 mL	1 tsp	7 mL	1½ tsp
Oil	15 mL	1 tbsp	25 mL	2 tbsp
Honey	25 mL	2 tbsp	35 mL	3 tbsp
Water	250 mL	1 cup	325 mL	1⅓ cups
Yeast	7 mL	1½ tsp	10 mL	2 tsp

tip

Gluten IV *Buy about 100 to 200 g (3 to 6 oz) gluten to keep on hand for restoring old wheat flour. When you have a recipe that doesn't work because the gluten seems to have dissipated from the whole wheat flour, add 5 to 10 mL (1 to 2 tsp) of gluten the next time you use that flour. Store gluten in a sealed container in the refrigerator.*

Buttermilk Loaf

With the subtle flavour of whole wheat, this recipe is suitable for every type of bread machine.

	Small Loaf		Large Loaf	
All-purpose flour	200 mL	¾ cup	300 mL	1¼ cups
Whole wheat flour	250 mL	1 cup	375 mL	1½ cups
Cornmeal	50 mL	¼ cup	75 mL	⅓ cup
Salt	5 mL	1 tsp	7 mL	1½ tsp
Sugar	15 mL	1 tbsp	25 mL	2 tbsp
Oil	15 mL	1 tbsp	25 mL	2 tbsp
Buttermilk	250 mL	1 cup	375 mL	1½ cups
Yeast	5 mL	1 tsp	7 mL	1½ tsp

tip

Buttermilk   *If you enjoy this loaf, keep powdered buttermilk on hand. Mix 50 mL (¼ cup) with water to equal 250 mL (1 cup) and 75 mL (⅓ cup) to make 375 mL (1½ cups).*

Cracked Wheat Loaf

For extra fibre try this light loaf, which is ideal for toast with honey.

	Small Loaf			Large Loaf		
All-purpose flour	250	mL	1 cup	375	mL	1½ cups
Whole wheat flour	200	mL	¾ cup	300	mL	1⅓ cups
Cracked wheat	50	mL	¼ cup	75	mL	⅓ cup
Salt	5	mL	1 tsp	7	mL	1½ tsp
Brown sugar	15	mL	1 tbsp	25	mL	2 tbsp
Oil	15	mL	1 tbsp	25	mL	2 tbsp
Water	200	mL	¾ cup	300	mL	1⅓ cups
Yeast	5	mL	1 tsp	7	mL	1½ tsp

tip

Flour IV *When bread containing whole wheat flour fails to rise, the first thing you should do is check the age and condition of the flour. If whole wheat flour has not been stored under ideal cool conditions, enzymes that interfere with the action of the yeast may develop in the germ. Try the same recipe with new flour.*

50% Whole Wheat

Even if your bread machine does not have a whole wheat cycle, you can get a good whole wheat loaf from this recipe.

	Small Loaf		Large Loaf	
All-purpose flour	250 mL	1 cup	375 mL	1½ cups
Whole wheat flour	250 mL	1 cup	375 mL	1½ cups
Cornmeal	25 mL	2 tbsp	50 mL	¼ cup
Salt	5 mL	1 tsp	7 mL	1½ tsp
Sugar	5 mL	1 tsp	10 mL	2 tsp
Oil	15 mL	1 tbsp	25 mL	2 tbsp
Molasses	10 mL	2 tsp	15 mL	1 tbsp
Water	225 mL	¾ cup	350 mL	1¼ cups
Yeast	5 mL	1 tsp	7 mL	1½ tsp

tip

Flour V   *It is not always easy to determine the freshness of flour. If you shop in the same store regularly, you can get to know their stock and speed of turnover. Ask the manager for the milling date. If he or she knows, you are in luck; very few stores know the age of the flour they sell. All-purpose flour keeps for 10 to 12 months, while whole wheat flour keeps for three months.*

Ginger Wheat Loaf

A hint of ginger tickles your nose when this loaf is baking. It's great for toast, too.

	Small Loaf		Large Loaf	
All-purpose flour	250 mL	1 cup	375 mL	1½ cups
Whole wheat flour	250 mL	1 cup	375 mL	1½ cups
Candied chopped ginger	15 mL	1 tbsp	25 mL	2 tbsp
Margarine or butter	15 mL	1 tbsp	25 mL	2 tbsp
Brown sugar	10 mL	2 tsp	15 mL	1 tbsp
Salt	5 mL	1 tsp	7 mL	1½ tsp
Grated lemon peel	5 mL	1 tsp	7 mL	1½ tsp
Lemon juice	10 mL	2 tsp	15 mL	1 tbsp
Mace	pinch	pinch	pinch	pinch
Egg plus	1	1	1	1
Milk or water to equal	200 mL	⅔ cup	275 mL	1¼ cups
Yeast	5 mL	1 tsp	7 mL	1½ tsp

Honey Wheat Bread

Traditional flavour with a light texture. Enjoyed even by people who only fancy white bread.

	Small Loaf		Large Loaf	
Whole wheat flour	375 mL	1½ cups	500 mL	2 cups
All-purpose flour	125 mL	½ cup	250 mL	1 cup
Nutmeg	1 mL	¼ tsp	2 mL	½ tsp
Salt	5 mL	1 tsp	7 mL	1½ tsp
Margarine or butter	15 mL	1 tbsp	25 mL	2 tbsp
Honey	15 mL	1 tbsp	25 mL	2 tbsp
Egg plus	1	1	1	1
Water to equal	200 mL	¾ cup	300 mL	1¼ cups
Yeast	5 mL	1 tsp	7 mL	1½ tsp

Multi-Grain Loaf

Twelve grains give a nutty flavour that will impress the lunch-box set.

	Small Loaf		Large Loaf	
All-purpose flour	400 mL	1½ cups	625 mL	2⅓ cups
Barley flour	75 mL	⅓ cup	125 mL	½ cup
12-grain cereal	50 mL	¼ cup	75 mL	⅓ cup
Salt	5 mL	1 tsp	7 mL	1½ tsp
Brown sugar	15 mL	1 tbsp	25 mL	2 tbsp
Oil	15 mL	1 tbsp	25 mL	2 tbsp
Water	225 mL	⅞ cup	325 mL	1⅓ cups
Yeast	5 mL	1 tsp	7 mL	1½ tsp

tip

Measuring III   *Make measuring less messy by either putting a sheet of waxed paper on the counter or have canisters with large openings so that the tops of measuring cups and spoons can be levelled off over them.*

Prairie Brown Bread

This light loaf is delicious for toast and sandwiches because of the added texture rolled oats provides.

	Small Loaf		Large Loaf	
All-purpose flour	250 mL	1 cup	375 mL	1½ cups
Whole wheat flour	125 mL	½ cup	250 mL	1 cup
Rolled oats	125 mL	½ cup	200 mL	⅔ cup
Salt	5 mL	1 tsp	7 mL	1½ tsp
Oil	15 mL	1 tbsp	25 mL	2 tbsp
Molasses	10 mL	2 tsp	15 mL	1 tbsp
Water	225 mL	1 cup	350 mL	1⅓ cups
Yeast	5 mL	1 tsp	7 mL	1½ tsp

Bacon and Egg Loaf

The eggs and bacon are ideal when you don't have time for a full breakfast.

	Small Loaf		Large Loaf	
All-purpose flour	375 mL	1½ cups	500 mL	2 cups
Whole wheat flour	125 mL	½ cup	250 mL	1 cup
Cooked bacon pieces	25 mL	2 tbsp	50 mL	¼ cup
Chopped green pepper	25 mL	2 tbsp	50 mL	¼ cup
Black pepper	dash	dash	dash	dash
Salt	1 mL	¼ tsp	2 mL	½ tsp
Sugar	5 mL	1 tsp	7 mL	1½ tsp
Margarine	10 mL	2 tsp	15 mL	1 tbsp
Egg	1	1	1	1
Yogurt	75 mL	⅓ cup	100 mL	⅓ cup
Milk	100 mL	½ cup	200 mL	⅔ cup
Yeast	5 mL	1 tsp	7 mL	1½ tsp

Linseed Loaf

Linseed with its nutty flavour is among many foods that contribute to good health.

	Small Loaf		Large Loaf	
All-purpose flour	125 mL	½ cup	250 mL	1 cup
Whole wheat flour	375 mL	1½ cups	500 mL	2 cups
Salt	5 mL	1 tsp	7 mL	1½ tsp
Brown sugar	15 mL	1 tbsp	25 mL	2 tbsp
Flax seeds (linseed)	15 mL	1 tbsp	25 mL	2 tbsp
Oil or margarine	15 mL	1 tbsp	25 mL	2 tbsp
Water or milk	225 mL	⅞ cup	300 mL	1¼ cups
Yeast	5 mL	1 tsp	7 mL	1½ tsp

Sprouted Grain Loaf

When you like grains yet prefer less crunch, try sprouting them first.

	Small Loaf		Large Loaf	
Whole wheat flour	375 mL	1½ cups	500 mL	2 cups
All-purpose flour	75 mL	⅓ cup	125 mL	½ cup
Kamut or millet flour	75 mL	⅓ cup	125 mL	½ cup
Sprouted grain	75 mL	⅓ cup	125 mL	½ cup
Salt	5 mL	1 tsp	7 mL	1½ tsp
Sugar	15 mL	1 tbsp	25 mL	2 tbsp
Oil	15 mL	1 tbsp	25 mL	2 tbsp
Water	250 mL	1 cup	325 mL	1¼ cups
Yeast	5 mL	1 tsp	7 mL	1½ tsp

tip: *To sprout grains: perforate the lid of a large jar or use a piece of cheesecloth secured with an elastic band. Measure amount of grain in recipe into jar and add double the amount of warm water. Cover with perforated lid or with a piece of cheesecloth. Drain and rinse twice daily for 3 to 4 days until sprouts show. Measure and use immediately in recipe.*

Seed Loaf

Seeds add texture to bread and even more flavour when toasted.

	Small Loaf		Large Loaf	
All-purpose flour	250 mL	1 cup	375 mL	1½ cups
Whole wheat flour	250 mL	1 cup	375 mL	1½ cups
Mace	0.5 mL	⅛ tsp	1 mL	¼ tsp
Salt	5 mL	1 tsp	7 mL	1½ tsp
Oil	15 mL	1 tbsp	25 mL	2 tbsp
Honey	15 mL	1 tbsp	25 mL	2 tbsp
Amaranth seeds	15 mL	1 tbsp	25 mL	2 tbsp
Sunflower seeds (unsalted)	50 mL	¼ cup	75 mL	1/3 cup
Water	175 mL	⅞ cup	300 mL	1¼ cups
Yeast	5 mL	1 tsp	7 mL	1½ tsp

tip

Bread Crumbs   *Save bread crusts and old slices. Break up the pieces and store in an open bowl in a dry place. When the bread has dried, crush it in your food processor, blender or place in a plastic or paper bag and crush with a rolling pin or hammer, to make the most wonderful flavoured bread crumbs.*

Caraway Rye

This is the typical flavour of rye bread we are accustomed to. Slice thinly to enjoy the low, dense loaf.

	Small Loaf		Large Loaf	
All-purpose flour	375 mL	1½ cup	550 mL	2⅔ cups
Rye flour	125 mL	½ cup	250 mL	1 cup
Salt	2 mL	½ tsp	5 mL	1 tsp
Caraway seeds	2 mL	½ tsp	5 mL	1 tsp
Oil	15 mL	1 tbsp	25 mL	2 tbsp
Molasses	15 mL	1 tbsp	25 mL	2 tbsp
Beer and/or water	225 mL	¾ cup	341 mL*	1⅓ cups
Yeast	5 mL	1 tsp	7 mL	1½ tsp

*One bottle of beer

tip

Bread Flour   *Bread flour does make exceptional bread, so if you find it readily available and at the right price, by all means use it.*

Old World Rye

A fine-grained loaf is produced by the combination of grains. This is my favourite toasted with honey and peanut butter.

	Small Loaf		Large Loaf	
All-purpose flour	375 mL	1½ cups	625 mL	2½ cups
Rye flour	125 mL	½ cup	125 mL	½ cup
Buckwheat flour	50 mL	¼ cup	75 mL	⅓ cup
Salt	5 mL	1 tsp	7 mL	1½ tsp
Oil	15 mL	1 tbsp	25 mL	2 tbsp
Molasses or brown sugar	10 mL	2 tsp	15 mL	1 tbsp
Buttermilk	225 mL	1 cup	350 mL	1⅓ cups
Yeast	5 mL	1 tsp	7 mL	1½ tsp

Onion Rye

The great flavour in this dense loaf comes from frying the onions in the margarine before adding both to the other ingredients.

	Small Loaf		Large Loaf	
All-purpose flour	375 mL	1½ cups	550 mL	2¼ cups
Rye flour	125 mL	½ cup	200 mL	¾ cup
Salt	5 mL	1 tsp	7 mL	1½ tsp
Chopped onions	50 mL	¼ cup	75 mL	⅓ cup
Margarine	15 mL	1 tbsp	25 mL	2 tbsp
Molasses	10 mL	2 tsp	15 mL	1 tbsp
Milk or water	200 mL	¾ cup	325 mL	1¼ cups
Yeast	5 mL	1 tsp	7 mL	1½ tsp

Suomi Rye Loaf

This bread is based on a combination of ingredients that is a favourite of the Finns.

	Small Loaf		Large Loaf	
All-purpose flour	375 mL	1½ cups	550 mL	2¼ cups
Rye flour	125 mL	½ cup	200 mL	¾ cup
Whole bean flour or barley flour	50 mL	¼ cup	75 mL	⅓ cup
Rolled oats	50 mL	¼ cup	75 mL	⅓ cup
Gluten	15 mL	1 tbsp	25 mL	2 tbsp
Salt	5 mL	1 tsp	7 mL	1½ tsp
Brown sugar	15 mL	1 tbsp	25 mL	2 tbsp
Margarine or butter	15 mL	1 tbsp	25 mL	2 tbsp
Water or milk	250 mL	1 cup	350 mL	1⅓ cups
Yeast	5 mL	1 tsp	7 mL	1½ tsp

SWEETS WITH YEAST

Here are a few recipes where you can get a sweet loaf without going to all the bother of making a shaped loaf. There are a variety of textures, flavours and aromas in these sweets with yeast.

Basic Sweet Loaf

This is great thickly sliced just with butter and wonderful toasted as a snack or even as dessert. Get inspired and try your own variations.

	Small Loaf		Large Loaf	
All-purpose flour	500 mL	2 cups	750 mL	3 cups
Cinnamon	2 mL	½ tsp	5 mL	1 tsp
Salt	5 mL	1 tsp	7 mL	1½ tsp
Grated lemon peel	5 mL	1 tsp	7 mL	1½ tsp
Lemon juice	5 mL	1 tsp	7 mL	1½ tsp
Sugar	25 mL	2 tbsp	35 mL	3 tbsp
Egg plus	1	1	1	1
milk to equal	225 mL	⅞ cup	350 mL	1⅓ cups
Yeast	5 mL	1 tsp	7 mL	1½ tsp

Variations

Raisin Loaf:

Add very dry raisins	50 mL	¼ cup	75 mL	⅓ cup

Apricot Loaf:

Add chopped dried apricots	50 mL	¼ cup	75 mL	⅓ cup

Babka

Enjoy the flavour of Polish Easter bread for a special treat, without using the time required to make the traditional version.

	Small Loaf		Large Loaf	
All-purpose flour	375 mL	1½ cups	500 mL	2 cups
Grated lemon peel	2 mL	½ tsp	5 mL	1 tsp
Lemon juice	2 mL	½ tsp	5 mL	1 tsp
Sugar	35 mL	3 tbsp	50 mL	¼ cup
Butter or margarine	50 mL	¼ cup	75 mL	⅓ cup
Egg yolks	2	2	4	4
Sour cream	35 mL	3 tbsp	50 mL	¼ cup
Milk	75 mL	⅓ cup	100 mL	⅓ cup
Yeast	7 mL	1½ tsp	10 mL	2 tsp
Raisins, white*	25 mL	2 tbsp	35 mL	3 tbsp

*Raisins are traditionally optional. Try Babka both ways using your "add ingredients" signal to put the raisins into the bread pan at the correct time.

Babka is also delicious iced while it is still warm so the icing runs down the sides. Try the following glaze.

Runny Lemon Glaze

Icing sugar	250 mL	1 cup
Water	25 mL	2 tbsp
Lemon juice	5 mL	1 tsp

Mix ingredients in a small bowl until smooth and spoon over the loaf.

---

tip

Egg Whites *Save the egg whites to add to scrambled eggs or place in a clean glass jar, seal and freeze to use for angel food cake, macaroons or fat-free baking.*

Coconut Peach Bread

Peaches and coconut give a tantalizing hint of summer all year long.

	Small Loaf		Large Loaf	
All-purpose flour	500 mL	2 cups	750 mL	3 cups
Unsweetened shredded coconut	50 mL	¼ cup	75 mL	⅓ cup
Canned peaches, drained	125 mL	½ cup	200 mL	¾ cup
Cinnamon or allspice	1 mL	¼ tsp	2 mL	½ tsp
Salt	5 mL	1 tsp	7 mL	1½ tsp
Margarine or butter	15 mL	1 tbsp	25 mL	2 tbsp
Almond extract	1 drop	1 drop	2 drops	2 drops
Coconut milk or water	125 mL	½ cup	175 mL	⅔ cup
Peach syrup	50 mL	¼ cup	75 mL	⅓ cup
Yeast	5 mL	1 tsp	7 mL	1½ tsp

tip

Canned Fruit   *When adding canned fruit or vegetables to a recipe, drain them in a sieve to make them as dry as possible before putting into the bread pan, otherwise your dough will be too soft.*

Cranberry-Apple Loaf

The blush of apple is enhanced by leaving on the peel, which adds fibre as well. Check the dough ball while making this recipe because the moisture content in apples can vary.

	Small Loaf		Large Loaf	
All-purpose flour	500 mL	2 cups	750 mL	3 cups
Cranberries (fresh or frozen) and chopped apples to equal	125 mL	½ cup	175 mL	⅔ cup
Cinnamon	5 mL	1 tsp	7 mL	1½ tsp
Salt	5 mL	1 tsp	7 mL	1½ tsp
Brown sugar	25 mL	2 tbsp	35 mL	3 tbsp
Margarine	15 mL	1 tbsp	25 mL	2 tbsp
Egg plus	1	1	1	1
Apple juice to equal	175 mL	⅔ cup	250 mL	1 cup
Yeast	5 mL	1 tsp	7 mL	1½ tsp

tip

Humidity   *If it is a warm summer day when you first start using the recipes from this book, you may need to adjust the amount of liquid to compensate for the humidity that the flour absorbs. I suggest you start with a simple loaf, make it on the shortest cycle and check the dough when it first starts kneading. This way you can check whether or not the dough is too soft. If the humidity is high, you may wish to set aside about two spoonfuls of liquid from the recipe in a cup. It can be poured onto the dough ball in the pan later, if required. Remember, it is much easier to add liquid than flour.*

Orange-Cocoa Loaf

This sweet treat without the high calories of cake is great for cocoa lovers.

	Small Loaf		Large Loaf	
All-purpose flour	500 mL	2 cups	750 mL	3 cups
Cocoa	50 mL	¼ cup	75 mL	⅓ cup
Salt	5 mL	1 tsp	7 mL	1½ tsp
Grated orange peel	5 mL	1 tsp	10 mL	2 tsp
Sugar	50 mL	¼ cup	75 mL	⅓ cup
Butter or margarine	25 mL	2 tbsp	35 mL	3 tbsp
Egg plus	1	1	1	1
Milk to equal	225 mL	⅞ cup	325 mL	1¼ cups
Yeast	5 mL	1 tsp	7 mL	1½ tsp

tip

Flour VI   *Try to keep track of how much flour you use in a month. That way you can purchase only what is required and keep your supply fresh.*

Peanut Butter and Banana Loaf

A true peanut butter lover would use crunchy peanut butter to make this bread even more peanutty.

	Small Loaf		Large Loaf	
All-purpose flour	500 mL	2 cups	750 mL	3 cups
Peanut butter	50 mL	¼ cup	75 mL	⅓ cup
Nutmeg	2 mL	½ tsp	5 mL	1 tsp
Salt	5 mL	1 tsp	7 mL	1½ tsp
Brown sugar	15 mL	1 tbsp	25 mL	2 tbsp
Milk	150 mL	⅔ cup	225 mL	1 cup
Banana*	100 mL	⅓ cup	150 mL	½ cup
Yeast	5 mL	1 tsp	7 mL	1½ tsp

*Put milk in cup accurately measured, then add cut-up bananas until you have the total amount of the two ingredients.

Saint Lucia Loaf

Traditionally made as buns for the Festival of Lights in Sweden, on December 13, this loaf is a simple but mouth-watering substitute. It is traditionally drizzled with vanilla icing.

	Small Loaf		Large Loaf	
All-purpose flour	500 mL	2 cups	750 mL	3 cups
Cardamom seeds	0.5 mL	⅛ tsp	1 mL	¼ tsp
Saffron threads	1 mL	¼ tsp	2 mL	½ tsp
Salt	5 mL	1 tsp	7 mL	1½ tsp
Grated lemon peel	5 mL	1 tsp	7 mL	1½ tsp
Lemon juice	5 mL	1 tsp	7 mL	1½ tsp
Sugar	15 mL	1 tbsp	25 mL	2 tbsp
Raisins	50 mL	¼ cup	75 mL	⅓ cup
Butter or margarine	15 mL	1 tbsp	25 mL	2 tbsp
Egg plus	1	1	1	1
Milk to equal	225 mL	¾ cup	325 mL	1¼ cups
Yeast	5 mL	1 tsp	7 mL	1½ tsp

Vanilla Icing

Icing sugar	250 mL	1 cup
Milk	25 mL	2 tbsp
Vanilla	5 mL	1 tsp

Mix ingredients in a small bowl until smooth and spoon over loaf.

Strawberry Loaf

This is the best bread to use for cream cheese sandwiches, whether open-faced or closed. The contrasting colours announce the delicious flavours. A few sliced berries would add the perfect garnish.

	Small Loaf		Large Loaf	
All-purpose flour	500 mL	2 cups	750 mL	3 cups
Black pepper	dash	dash	dash	dash
Salt	5 mL	1 tsp	7 mL	1½ tsp
Grated lemon peel	5 mL	1 tsp	7 mL	1½ tsp
Sugar	25 mL	2 tbsp	35 mL	3 tbsp
Margarine	25 mL	2 tbsp	35 mL	3 tbsp
Chopped hazelnuts	25 mL	2 tbsp	50 mL	¼ cup
Mashed strawberries* plus water to equal	250 mL	1 cup	375 mL	1½ cups
Yeast	5 mL	1 tsp	7 mL	1½ tsp

This dough starts out very dry until the strawberries have worked into the flour and moistened it completely.

*When measuring berries, the water should just fill the spaces between the strawberries, so make sure you use lots of fruit. In the off-season, use frozen berries, measuring them while there are still ice crystals in them and omitting the water, since these berries are very wet.

Maple Walnut Loaf

Here is the most Canadian of flavours, in a loaf that is great with butter and honey or toasted.

	Small Loaf		Large Loaf	
All-purpose flour	450 mL	1¾ cups	675 mL	2¾ cups
Buckwheat flour	50 mL	¼ cup	75 mL	⅓ cup
Chopped walnuts	50 mL	¼ cup	75 mL	⅓ cup
Salt	5 mL	1 tsp	7 mL	1½ tsp
Butter or margarine	15 mL	1 tbsp	25 mL	2 tbsp
Maple syrup	15 mL	1 tbsp	25 mL	2 tbsp
Brown sugar	5 mL	1 tsp	15 mL	1 tbsp
Water	200 mL	¾ cup	300 mL	1¼ cups
Yeast	5 mL	1 tsp	7 mL	1½ tsp

Lemon Poppy Seed Loaf

Poppy seeds give crunch and sweetness to this rich bread, which makes a great gift.

	Small Loaf		Large Loaf	
All-purpose flour	500 mL	2 cups	750 mL	3 cups
Chopped almonds	50 mL	¼ cup	75 mL	⅓ cup
Salt	2 mL	½ tsp	5 mL	1 tsp
Grated lemon peel	10 mL	2 tsp	15 mL	1 tbsp
Lemon juice	15 mL	1 tbsp	25 mL	2 tbsp
Poppy seeds	15 mL	1 tbsp	25 mL	2 tbsp
Brown sugar	35 mL	3 tbsp	50 mL	¼ cup
Butter or margarine	25 mL	2 tbsp	35 mL	3 tbsp
Egg plus	1	1	1	1
Milk to equal	200 mL	¾ cup	300 mL	1¼ cups
Yeast	5 mL	1 tsp	7 mL	1½ tsp

Challah (Egg Loaf)

It's a wonderful loaf for brunch instead of sweet cake. The egg adds to the soft cakelike texture.

	Small Loaf		Large Loaf	
All-purpose flour	500 mL	2 cups	750 mL	3 cups
Salt	5 mL	1 tsp	7 mL	1½ tsp
Sugar	25 mL	2 tbsp	35 mL	3 tbsp
Butter	25 mL	2 tbsp	35 mL	3 tbsp
Egg plus	1	1	2	2
Milk to equal	250 mL	1 cup	325 mL	1¼ cups
Yeast	2 mL	½ tsp	5 mL	1 tsp

Remove from pan when hot, rub loaf with butter or margarine and sprinkle with sesame or poppy seeds.

SOURDOUGH BREADS

In the days before yeast was available in the local store, home bakers made their own starter, as they called it, by fermenting flour and raw potato in warm water. They used small portions of starter in making bread and as the supply dwindled, made new starter using bread dough and old starter as a base. A starter was so important to early Canadians that when prospectors and hunters set off into the wilderness, they carried a little piece of it inside their coat, safe and at the right temperature.

In the 1920s, when commercial yeast became available in stores, homemakers no longer needed to make their own starter. But people had grown to like the distinctive taste of bread made with traditional starter, and it became known as sourdough bread.

The flavour of sourdough bread varies in different areas of the country because of the microscopic spores that react with the starter. Unless you live along the seacoast, your bread cannot naturally develop the traditional flavour of San Francisco sourdough. In Canada, the equivalent effect is available in Vancouver, where the sea atmosphere contributes a unique flavour. Commercial bakeries in other areas use chemical additives to duplicate the flavour.

Bread machines were not developed for use with starters so some adjustments are required. I do not recommend any starter recipe other than those I have provided. Make a new batch each time since the yeast in starters can grow in a wild and unpredictable manner, and you cannot expect the same results every time. Sometimes they are fantastic and at other times the bread will mushroom before baking. As well, off-odours and flavours can result. The starters in this book impart the distinctive sourdough flavour. They will be consistent because of the inclusion of instant or active dry commercial yeast.

Starters should be kept in a cool place below 20°C (71°F) and not stirred while they are developing.

If you do not use the starter as soon as it is ready, refrigerate it for up to 2 days. However, if the colour changes to orange or the aroma is not the familiar slightly sour one when you take it out to use, or it grows out of the container, popping the lid, throw it away and make fresh starter.

THREE STARTERS

All-Purpose Starter

	Small		Large	
Yield	200 mL	¾ cup	250 mL	1 cup
All-purpose flour	125 mL	½ cup	175 mL	⅔ cup
Warm water	125 mL	½ cup	175 mL	⅔ cup
Yeast	2 mL	½ tsp	2 mL	½ tsp

Put ingredients in a 750 g or 1 litre (1 quart) glass or plastic container with a loose lid. Stir and leave at room temperature for 2 days.

Whole Wheat Starter

	Small		Large	
Yield	175 mL	⅔ cup	225 mL	¾ cup
Whole wheat flour	125 mL	½ cup	175 mL	⅔ cup
Warm water	125 mL	½ cup	175 mL	⅔ cup
Yeast	2 mL	½ tsp	2 mL	½ tsp

Put ingredients in a 750 g or 1 litre (1 quart) glass or plastic container with a loose lid. Stir and leave at room temperature for 2 days.

Rye Starter

	Small		Large	
Yield	175 mL	⅔ cup	225 mL	⅞ cup
Rye flour	125 mL	½ cup	175 mL	⅔ cup
Warm water	125 mL	½ cup	175 mL	⅔ cup
Yeast	2 mL	½ tsp	2 mL	½ tsp
Onion slice	1	1	1	1

Put flour, warm water and yeast in a 750 g or 1 litre (1 quart) glass or plastic container with a loose lid. Stir, add onion slice and leave at room temperature for 1 day. Remove onion slice and leave for up to 2 days.

SOURDOUGH LOAVES

Sourdough White Loaf

A light texture and slightly tart flavour are the result of using a starter.

	Small Loaf		Large Loaf	
All-purpose starter	200 mL	¾ cup	250 mL	1 cup
All-purpose flour	375 mL	1 ½ cups	625 mL	2⅔ cups
Salt	5 mL	1 tsp	7 mL	1 ½ tsp
Sugar	15 mL	1 tbsp	25 mL	2 tbsp
Oil	15 mL	1 tbsp	25 mL	2 tbsp
Water	75 mL	⅓ cup	175 mL	⅔ cup
Yeast	4 mL	¾ tsp	5 mL	1 tsp

Sourdough Oatmeal Loaf

A flavour reminiscent of Scottish oatcakes and a light texture enjoyed by all.

	Small Loaf		*Large Loaf*	
All-purpose starter	200 mL	¾ cup	250 mL	1 cup
Rolled oats	125 mL	½ cup	200 mL	¾ cup
All-purpose flour	350 mL	1⅓ cups	550 mL	2¼ cups
Salt	5 mL	1 tsp	7 mL	1½ tsp
Oil	15 mL	1 tbsp	25 mL	2 tbsp
Honey	10 mL	2 tsp	15 mL	1 tbsp
Water	75 mL	⅓ cup	125 mL	½ cup
Yeast	4 mL	¾ tsp	5 mL	1 tsp

Sourdough Whole Wheat Loaf

You are sure to enjoy this version of whole wheat bread if you are fond of the nutty flavour the wheat bran provides.

	Small Loaf		*Large Loaf*	
Whole wheat starter	175 mL	⅔ cup	225 mL	¾ cup
Whole wheat flour	375 mL	1½ cups	500 mL	2 cups
All-purpose flour	75 mL	⅓ cup	175 mL	⅔ cup
Salt	5 mL	1 tsp	7 mL	1½ tsp
Brown sugar	15 mL	1 tbsp	25 mL	2 tbsp
Oil	15 mL	1 tbsp	25 mL	2 tbsp
Water	75 mL	⅓ cup	175 mL	⅔ cup
Yeast	4 mL	¾ tsp	5 mL	1 tsp

Sourdough Rye Loaf

A rye that is typically sour yet as light as the basic white loaves.

	Small Loaf		Large Loaf	
Rye starter	175 mL	⅔ cup	225 mL	⅞ cup
All-purpose flour	375 mL	1½ cups	550 mL	2¼ cups
Salt	5 mL	1 tsp	7 mL	1½ tsp
Oil	15 mL	1 tbsp	25 mL	2 tbsp
Molasses	15 mL	1 tbsp	25 mL	2 tbsp
Water or milk	75 mL	⅓ cup	175 mL	⅔ cup
Yeast	4 mL	¾ tsp	5 mL	1 tsp

Sourdough Corn Loaf

A sweet flavour is the result of corn flour. Buy white or yellow corn flour at your bulk food store.

	Small Loaf		Large Loaf	
All-purpose starter	175 mL	⅔ cup	250 mL	1 cup
All-purpose flour	325 mL	1¼ cups	500 mL	2 cups
Corn flour	125 mL	½ cup	200 mL	¾ cup
Salt	5 mL	1 tsp	7 mL	1½ tsp
Sugar	5 mL	1 tsp	7 mL	1½ tsp
Oil	15 mL	1 tbsp	25 mL	2 tbsp
Water	100 mL	⅓ cup	150 mL	½ cup
Yeast	2 mL	½ tsp	5 mL	1 tsp

SPECIAL LOAVES FOR SPECIAL PEOPLE

So many of us love the flavour and aroma of baking bread that, when there is an automatic bread machine in the house, our senses are stimulated and we may be tempted to eat the very foods we should avoid. But don't despair – here are a few recipes to help you stay within your diet.

Salt-Free Loaves

Salt-free bread is easy: simply leave the salt out of any recipe. The cell structure in the bread may be coarser, but you will have real bread. To prevent over-rising in sweet breads, reduce the sugar by half and omit the salt.

Salt-Free Grain Loaf

The ingredients in this bread compensate for the lack of salt.

	Small Loaf		Large Loaf	
All-purpose flour	400 mL	1½ cups	600 mL	2⅓ cups
Five-grain cereal	75 mL	⅓ cup	125 mL	½ cup
Spelt flour	50 mL	¼ cup	75 mL	⅓ cup
Grated lemon peel	5 mL	1 tsp	7 mL	1½ tsp
Brown sugar	15 mL	1 tbsp	25 mL	2 tbsp
Oil or margarine	15 mL	1 tbsp	25 mL	2 tbsp
Water or milk	250 mL	1 cup	375 mL	1⅓ cups
Yeast	5 mL	1 tsp	7 mL	1½ tsp

Salt-Free Millet Loaf

Millet flour and the coarser ground millet meal provide a cornlike flavour to compensate for the elimination of salt.

	Small Loaf		Large Loaf	
All-purpose flour	375 mL	1½ cups	550 mL	2¼ cups
Millet flour	125 mL	½ cup	200 mL	¾ cup
Millet meal	15 mL	1 tbsp	25 mL	2 tbsp
Sugar	15 mL	1 tbsp	25 mL	2 tbsp
Oil	15 mL	1 tbsp	25 mL	2 tbsp
Milk	225 mL	½ cup	300 mL	1⅓ cups
Yeast	5 mL	1 tsp	7 mL	1½ tsp

Egg-Free Loaves

Egg-free recipes are simple. All you have to do is to avoid recipes with eggs or arrange for a liquid substitution. For instance, "shapes" often have some egg in the recipe so you may use extra liquid instead of the egg. Most of the recipes here treat eggs as liquid for measuring purposes. The egg holds the dough together and gives it a different texture which will not be there without the egg. You may find the dough softer, so knead more flour into it before shaping.

Milk-Free Loaves

Milk-free recipes are the simplest of all since they can be made with water substituted for milk. Some people like to use milk substitutes such as soya or rice milk, which are equally successful. For those who like to cook with lactose-free milk, this can also be substituted.

Gluten-Free Loaves

Gluten-free bread is a challenge, since leavened bread requires gluten to make a traditional loaf. Still, good bread can be made without gluten, as the following recipes prove. Here are some tips for making gluten-free bread.

❖ Include the yeast with the dry ingredients so that it mixes completely, even if your bread machine has a yeast dispenser.

❖ Use a rubber spatula to mix ingredients in the bread pan to avoid scratching the nonstick surface.

❖ Mix the dry ingredients in the pan and use an extra-large measuring cup for the liquid ingredients. **You will notice the dry and liquid ingredients are separated in the recipe list.** Should the mix be too dry to stir, add some warm water to it, by the spoonful. The mixture should not be too wet, but soft enough to allow for proper stirring.

❖ The bread will not rise above 10 cm (4 in) and the top will be quite flat and cannot brown very much if your bread pan is deep. Do not double the recipe as the mixture will be too heavy to rise.

❖ Set your machine to the short or rapid cycle. Cool the loaf completely before slicing or storing.

Apple Cinnamon Loaf

Apple and cinnamon are a nice change from regular bread. Guar gum, a powder that substitutes for gluten, is the important ingredient.

Rice flour	375	mL	1½ cups
Tapioca starch	125	mL	½ cup
Salt	5	mL	1 tsp
Cinnamon	5	mL	1 tsp
Yeast	10	mL	2 tsp
Guar gum	15	mL	1 tbsp
Sugar	25	mL	2 tbsp
Milk	250	mL	1 cup
Apple juice	200	mL	¾ cup
Oil	15	mL	1 tbsp

Cassava Rice Loaf

The flavour of cassava is sweet like tapioca and blends well with the sharpness of quinoa.

White rice flour	375	mL	1½ cups
Cassava flour	125	mL	½ cup
Quinoa flour	50	mL	¼ cup
Salt	5	mL	1 tsp
Gelatin	5	mL	1 tsp
Yeast	10	mL	2 tsp
Sugar	15	mL	1 tbsp
Guar gum	15	mL	1 tbsp
Milk	550	mL	2¼ cups
Oil	15	mL	1 tbsp

Corn Loaf

A mellow flavour balanced with corn and bean flour provides variety.

Corn flour	250	mL	1 cup
Cornstarch	125	mL	½ cup
Whole bean flour	125	mL	½ cup
Cornmeal	50	mL	¼ cup
Salt	7	mL	1½ tsp
Yeast	10	mL	2 tsp
Sugar	15	mL	1 tbsp
Guar gum	15	mL	1 tbsp
Water	400	mL	1⅔ cups
Oil	15	mL	1 tbsp
Lemon juice	15	mL	1 tbsp
Egg	1		1

Corn-Potato-Buckwheat Loaf

Potato starch and potato flour are not the same and cannot be used interchangeably.

Corn flour	375	mL	1¾	cups
Potato starch	125	mL	⅔	cup
Buckwheat cereal	50	mL	¼	cup
Yeast	5	mL	1	tsp
Salt	10	mL	1½	tsp
Xanthan gum	25	mL	2	tbsp
Sugar	50	mL	¼	cup
Water	400	mL	1⅔	cups
Oil	15	mL	1	tbsp
Vinegar	5	mL	1	tsp
Eggs	2		2	

Reprinted with permission from Matsushita Electric of Canada.

Millet Loaf

Use white or brown rice for a pleasant texture variation in this light-textured loaf.

Millet flour	125	mL	½	cup
Rice flour	125	mL	½	cup
Potato starch	75	mL	⅓	cup
Tapioca starch	50	mL	¼	cup
Salt	5	mL	1	tsp
Yeast	10	mL	2	tsp
Guar gum	15	mL	1	tbsp
Sugar	50	mL	¼	cup
Milk	225	mL	⅞	cup
Oil	25	mL	2	tbsp
Vinegar	5	mL	1	tsp
Lemon juice	5	mL	1	tsp
Eggs	2		2	

Multi-Mix Loaf

The texture of brown rice flour and the protein provided by bean flour makes this an excellent contribution to your special diet.

Brown rice flour	250 mL	1 cup
Potato flour	125 mL	½ cup
Whole bean flour	125 mL	½ cup
Salt	5 mL	1 tsp
Yeast	10 mL	2 tsp
Guar gum	15 mL	1 tbsp
Sugar	25 mL	2 tbsp
Water	500 mL	2 cups
Oil	15 mL	1 tbsp
Lemon juice	5 mL	1 tsp

Brown Rice Loaf

This loaf has excellent flavour with the added fibre of rice bran.

Brown rice flour	375 mL	1½ cups
Tapioca starch	125 mL	½ cup
Salt	5 mL	1 tsp
Gelatin	5 mL	1 tsp
Yeast	10 mL	2 tsp
Xanthan gum	15 mL	1 tbsp
Sugar	25 mL	2 tbsp
Water	250 mL	1 cup
Oil	15 mL	1 tbsp
Lemon juice	10 mL	2 tsp
Eggs	2	2

Rice Loaf

This is one of the nicest homemade, light-textured rice breads enjoyed for years by many on the special diet.

Rice flour	250	mL	1	cup
Potato starch	125	mL	½	cup
Skim milk powder	125	mL	½	cup
Cornstarch	50	mL	¼	cup
Salt	5	mL	1	tsp
Sugar	5	mL	1	tsp
Xanthan gum	7	mL	1½	tsp
Yeast	7	mL	1½	tsp
Water	300	mL	1¼	cups
Sour cream	50	mL	¼	cup
Margarine	15	mL	1	tbsp
Eggs	2		2	

Reprinted with permission from Donna Wall, *Gluten Free Anytime*.

Chapter Six

Hand-Shaped Breads and Rolls

*W*hile many people will use their bread machine only to bake fresh loaves, many exciting delicacies can be created by making the dough in your bread machine, then shaping and finishing it in the oven.

You can use the bread machine to prepare foolproof dough, without worrying about whether you have the right degree of elasticity and without the time-consuming work of kneading it.

I suggest that you start with a simple dough that can be used for plain round rolls. The same dough can become pizza crust or an exotic pita bread baked with aromatic herbs. Before long, you will be serving Scandinavian Coffee Cakes, Rhubarb Kuchen or Salmon Havarti Braid to family and friends.

Most bread machines have a dough cycle in which the ingredients are mixed and kneaded, then the warming element switches on at a low temperature to make the dough rise. The machine then switches off and signals that the dough is ready. Some machines, however, do not have a true dough cycle and if you do not stop the machine manually, it will continue and bake dough into a loaf. Read your instruction manual and check which type of machine you have.

Dough for these shaped loaves and rolls needs to rise twice. Dough will rise once in the bread machine and once on the baking sheet. For machines without a dough cycle, you'll have to remove the dough and bucket and put them in a warm place for the first rising, then shape and let rise again on the baking sheet.

SHAPING

While dough is rising, get your work surface ready. Prepare a cutting board or smooth countertop by washing it with soap and water and drying it completely. If you have chopped onions, garlic, chicken or anything that could contaminate the surface, be sure to clean it especially well with a chlorine bleach solution to remove bacteria, flavours and odours.

In selecting your working surface, you might be cutting, so do not use a surface that could be permanently damaged. You will also need to collect fillings and flavourings, and get out your rolling pin, knives, spatulas and any pans.

Sprinkle a little all-purpose flour over the dry work surface, the rolling pin and any knives you will be using. Smooth the flour over the surface, which should be at least 40 x 50 cm (17 x 20").

Now it's time to get the risen dough, which is light, airy and probably a little sticky. The best way to get risen dough out of the bread machine pan is to turn it over and let the dough fall onto the floured surface. An alternative method is to sprinkle some flour onto your hands and gently help the dough out. Remove the paddle and rod from the dough and put them aside.

Knead the dough a few times. To knead, push the dough flat with the heel of your hands then fold one side over, rotate one-quarter turn so the fold faces you and push down on the dough again. If it is too sticky, sprinkle with more flour and keep kneading until the stickiness has disappeared and dough is elastic and smooth.

Flouring *If your recipe contains rye or whole wheat flour, you can use it for kneading and coating the work surface and rolling pin. All-purpose flour is absorbed by dough much more easily than are the other flours. The flavour of the finished product is just as good if you use all-purpose flour in the kneading.*

Repeat until the dough is no longer sticky. It should not take long but do keep sprinkling flour on the board.

A simple way to divide dough in equal parts is to roll it in a log, then cut it in equal-length portions with a floured chef's knife. You can trust your eyes or use a ruler.

tip
Pizza Dough *For some breads such as pizza, it is traditional to coat your hands with oil instead of flour to handle the dough. I have always found this very messy, but where it is the preferred method I have mentioned it in the recipe.*

If dough has to be rolled in a rectangle, shape it in a square with your hands, then use the floured rolling pin to roll out the longer sides.

If you do not have a rolling pin, an empty vinegar or wine bottle makes a good substitute. You can also use your hands to pat the dough and stretch it in the required size, being sure to flour your hands and the board well.

Think ahead when spreading fillings on dough. If the dough needs to be sealed once it is filled, do not bring the filling right to the edge of the dough. Leave enough space to pinch the dough together without having the filling ooze out.

Spiral breads and swirled buns can often look better when more filling is used to cover an unfilled cut surface. You will see exactly where these bare spots are as you work. Don't eat that extra filling until you are sure it won't be needed.

PROVIDING A NICE WARM PLACE FOR THE DOUGH TO RISE

The warm area should be about 77 to 86°F (25 to 30°C), moist and draft free. Here are some suggestions to produce an ideal spot:

❖ An area warmed by the sun is ideal, although you don't want the sun to shine directly on the covered pan since it may actually start to cook the dough.

❖ A microwave oven can create the correct environment. Place about 500 mL (2 cups) of water in the microwave, bring it to the boil, then put in the pan of dough. Do not turn on power or the pan may cause arcing. If the oven cools and you need to warm up the cavity again, remove the pan and reboil the water.

❖ A gas oven with a pilot light is also an ideal spot.

❖ An electric or gas oven without a pilot light will provide the correct temperature if turned on to 350°F (180°C) for one minute, then turned off.

❖ Place a bowl of hot water on the bottom shelf of an oven and put the pan(s) on the top shelf. If the water cools before the dough is risen, you will have to reheat the water.

❖ Place a rack over a bowl of hot water. Put the pan of dough on the rack. Totally cover both the pan and the bowl with a clean cloth. If the water cools before the dough is risen, you may have to reheat the water.

MORE HINTS ON RISING

The dough has risen enough when it rises to the top of the pan, which takes from 30 to 60 minutes in the machine. Some machines knead a few strokes (like punching down the dough by hand) just before the completion signal. This has the effect of making it look as if the dough has not risen enough. Check your instruction manual for a detailed description of the dough cycle.

If your bread machine does not have a special dough cycle which allows the dough to rise in the machine, simply take the bread machine pan, cover it and choose one of the methods above, in Providing a Nice Warm Place for the Dough To Rise.

Turn the dough out of the pan, and punch it with your fists a few times to remove gas bubbles. It is important to knead out these bubbles before shaping the dough, otherwise your loaf or roll will have oversize air holes in it when baked.

AFTER SHAPING THE DOUGH

I have indicated the preferred shape and size of pan for each recipe here, but if you do not have one exactly as recommended, substitute the closest you have.

The best pans for baking are aluminum or cast iron; a dark surface produces better browning. A nonstick finish means easy cleanup, but a light coating of fat is needed to help the crust form. You may only have glass loaf pans, in which case use them.

Whenever possible, use solid shortening for greasing the sides and bottom of pans. It stays on the sides of the pan better and melts more slowly, lessening the chance of the dough sticking to the pan. If you have no solid shortening on hand, substitute margarine or lard.

Butter and oil should not be used for greasing the pans. Butter burns at the high temperatures used when baking bread and will produce a terrible odour. Oil bakes onto the pan where there is no food cover, forming a sticky film.

Take a small piece of waxed paper and rub it over the shortening, then take the waxed paper and rub it over the bottom and sides of the pan. This should leave a light but visible film of shortening.

I usually put a light film of oil on top of shaped dough. I find this keeps the dough elastic, so that it will rise more easily and not form cracks in the surface. If the shaped dough already has a topping, don't oil.

When the shaped dough is set out in the pan or on the sheet, cover it and put it in a warm place for the second rising. I have found that putting a piece of waxed paper or plastic wrap on top of the dough, then adding a tea towel or lightweight terry towel helps keep the dough warm. It not only helps the dough to rise evenly, but also keeps the cloth clean.

Shaped dough should rise until twice its original volume. This is easy to judge when the dough is in the pan, but may be more difficult to see when the dough is on a sheet and is growing wider as well as higher. The best way to test the dough is by pressing a chopstick or wooden spoon handle lightly into it. If the dough has risen enough, this hole will not fill in immediately. This second rising usually takes 30 to 60 minutes. Dough that has not risen enough will make a tough roll or loaf, so be patient.

If you have left the dough for the required time in a warm place but it has not risen as much as it should, leave it for another 30 minutes or so. If there is still no action, the yeast is probably stale. Although it may be painful, there is no alternative but to throw it out and start again.

OVEN LORE

You might begin with the best doughs and most delightful fillings, but if you are not using your oven properly you will not get the results you deserve.

First, you must know the true temperature of your oven. Very few oven controls are accurate. The good news is that the error is usually in the thermostat and the error is constant. So buy an oven thermometer and check the actual temperature of your oven when the controls are set to various temperatures. Write down the actual temperatures and the set temperatures and keep the list by your oven.

You know the oven was not hot enough if the rolls are wet and gummy inside and the outside is not that lovely golden brown.

You know the oven was too hot if the rolls are small, burnt and hard on the outside and over-chewy and gummy on the inside.

If you do not have an oven thermometer, you can still check your oven by trial and error and good observation. For instance, if items are browning well before the finish time, the temperature is likely too hot, so reduce it by 50°F (20°C). If the oven is not hot enough, the next time start your oven 50°F (20°C) higher.

An oven usually takes about 20 minutes to heat to the high temperature necessary for yeast baking.

Once the oven is warm and the rolls or loaves have completed rising, put the pan in the oven. If you have only one pan to put in, put it in the middle, so arrange the shelves accordingly before pre-heating the oven.

If you have two or more pans, place them on different shelves and stagger them so that air can circulate around them. In placing the shelves, be sure to leave enough height for rolls or loaves to rise. Remembering that the oven is hotter at the top, it is best to rearrange the pans during cooking so that they all get equal heat, or you can remove the top pan first.

If you are using baking sheets, make sure they are small enough to allow proper air flow at the sides, perhaps a fist-width of space on all four sides.

Follow the instructions for approximate baking times then use your eyes and nose.

Every item, whether rolls, loaves or cakes, should ideally turn a lovely golden brown. If you think that they are getting overdone, use your judgment and lower the heat. However, when the recipe contains a lot of sugar or there is a sweet topping, or you have used whole wheat and bran, you will find the rolls and loaves get a little darker.

Another way of telling whether an item is finished is to jiggle or shake the baking sheet. If the items move or lift off the surface, the bottom crust is baked.

To ensure that your baking stays crisp and does not develop a soggy undercrust, use wire racks to cool the delicacies that come out of the oven. Take food off the baking pan as soon as you can. You will find that baked items slide off quite easily. Be especially careful when taking long loaves and braids with toppings out of the pan; the topping can spill or the loaf may crack. If this happens, use icing or spreads to camouflage any imperfections.

Let all yeast products cool to room temperature before storing in plastic bags. Crusty rolls should be stored in paper bags.

VARIATIONS ON SHAPE

You can use Mix-and-Match Plain Dough (page 129), Whole Wheat Plain Dough (page 130), Low-Fat Plain Dough (page 129), roll recipes or Mix-and-Match Sweet Dough (page 136) for these shapes.

Round rolls: Divide dough in balls as in recipe. Roll balls in melted margarine or butter if you wish. Put balls into greased muffin pan or on baking sheet, or nestle together in cake pan for pull-apart buns. Brush lightly with oil and let rise again.

Filled round rolls: Divide dough in balls and flatten each one in palm of hand. Place about 15 mL (1 tbsp) of filling in middle of dough, fold corners over and pinch dough together over filling. Place upside down on greased pan. Brush lightly with oil and let rise again. This is a very popular shape for quick sweet rolls.

Cloverleaf rolls: Divide each dough ball in three equal pieces. Roll each piece and nestle three balls in each greased muffin cup.

Crescent rolls: For small recipe, roll out 1 circle of dough (for large recipe, 2 circles of dough) 3 mm (⅛") thick. Cut each circle in 8 to 10 wedges. Roll up wedges from wide end to point, curve ends in and place on a greased baking sheet. Brush lightly with oil and let rise.

Knots: Divide dough according to the recipe; roll each portion in log shape on floured surface or between your hands. Tie each log in a knot and place on a greased baking sheet. Brush lightly with oil and let rise.

Fan-tans: Roll dough in 3 mm (⅛") sheets. Cut dough in strips 4 cm (1½") wide. Brush with olive oil and sprinkle with herbs OR brush with melted margarine or butter. Stack six strips together; cut in 4 cm (1½") pieces. Place each piece in greased muffin cup, cut side down. Brush with oil and let rise.

Hamburger Buns

Once you make your own hamburger buns, store-bought ones will pale by comparison. The onion variety are a special treat at a barbecue.

	8 Buns		12 Buns	
All-purpose flour	500 mL	2 cups	750 mL	3 cups
Sugar	25 mL	2 tbsp	35 mL	3 tbsp
Salt	5 mL	1 tsp	7 mL	1½ tsp
Oil	15 mL	1 tbsp	25 mL	2 tbsp
Egg	1	1	1	1
Water	150 mL	½ cup	250 mL	⅞ cup
Yeast	5 mL	1 tsp	7 mL	1½ tsp

Divide dough and shape as round, flat rolls. Place on greased baking sheet(s), brush with oil, cover and let rise in warm place about 30 minutes. Brush with oil again, if desired. Bake in preheated 400°F (200°C) oven for 10 to 15 minutes, until lightly browned.

Variation: Onion Barbecue Buns

Chopped onions	100 mL	⅓ cup	150 mL	⅔ cup

Fry onions in oil from dough recipe before adding both to the remaining ingredients. Complete as above.

Rye Hamburger Buns

Rye flakes provide an interesting change in texture.

	8 Buns		12 Buns	
All-purpose flour	250 mL	1 cup	375 mL	1½ cups
Whole wheat flour	250 mL	1 cup	375 mL	1½ cups
Rye flakes	75 mL	⅓ cup	125 mL	½ cup
Brown sugar	15 mL	1 tbsp	25 mL	2 tbsp
Salt	5 mL	1 tsp	7 mL	1½ tsp
Oil	15 mL	1 tbsp	25 mL	2 tbsp
Milk or water	200 mL	¾ cup	300 mL	1¼ cups
Yeast	5 mL	1 tsp	7 mL	1½ tsp

Coarse salt, caraway seeds (optional)

Divide dough and shape as round, flat rolls. Place on greased baking sheet(s), brush with oil, cover and let rise in warm place about 30 minutes. Brush with oil again, if desired, and sprinkle with salt or seeds. Bake in preheated 400°F (200°C) oven for 10 to 15 minutes, until lightly browned.

Crusty Rolls

These are perfect to serve with salads or chili. Store in a paper bag to keep them crisp.

	10 Rolls		16 Rolls	
All-purpose flour	500 mL	2 cups	750 mL	3 cups
Sugar	5 mL	1 tsp	7 mL	1½ tsp
Oil	25 mL	2 tbsp	35 mL	3 tbsp
Egg white	1	1	1	1
Water	200 mL	¾ cup	300 mL	1¼ cups
Yeast	10 mL	2 tsp	12 mL	2½ tsp

Divide dough and shape as round rolls. Placed on greased baking sheet(s), cover and let rise in warm place about 30 minutes. Bake in preheated 450°F (230°C) oven for 10 to 12 minutes, until lightly browned.

---

tip

Egg Yolk   *Cover unused egg yolk with water in a small dish and refrigerate to use within 48 hours. Or you can freeze egg yolks, but before you do, determine whether you plan to use them in a savoury or sweet recipe. Mix each yolk with either 5 mL (1 tsp) salt OR sugar to preserve them.*

Garlic Potato Rolls

These rolls are light even before baking, so handle dough carefully.

	10 Rolls		16 Rolls	
All-purpose flour	450 mL	1¾ cups	675 mL	2⅔ cups
Mashed potatoes*	125 mL	½ cup	200 mL	¾ cup
Barley flour	50 mL	¼ cup	75 mL	1/3 cup
Chopped fresh parsley	15 mL	1 tbsp	25 mL	2 tbsp
Salt	5 mL	1 tsp	7 mL	1½ tsp
Sugar	5 mL	1 tsp	7 mL	1½ tsp
Minced garlic	5 mL	1 tsp	7 mL	1½ tsp
Potato water, water or milk	200 mL	¾ cup	300 mL	1¼ cups
Yeast	5 mL	1 tsp	7 mL	1½ tsp

*If using instant mashed potato flakes:

	75 mL	⅓ cup	125 mL	½ cup

Divide dough evenly and shape as round balls. Place on greased baking sheet(s), cover and let rise in warm place about 30 minutes. Bake in preheated 375°F (190°C) oven 15 to 20 minutes, until browned.

Milk Rolls

Shaped as cloverleaf rolls, this light, delicately flavoured dough is perfect for a special lunch.

	10 Rolls		*16 Rolls*	
All-purpose flour	500 mL	2 cups	750 mL	3 cups
Mashed potatoes*	125 mL	½ cup	200 mL	¾ cup
Sugar	15 mL	1 tbsp	25 mL	2 tbsp
Salt	7 mL	1½ tsp	10 mL	2 tsp
Margarine or butter	15 mL	1 tbsp	25 mL	2 tbsp
Milk	175 mL	⅔ cup	275 mL	1¼ cup
Yeast	5 mL	1 tsp	7 mL	1½ tsp

*If using instant mashed potato flakes:

	75 mL	⅓ cup	125 mL	½ cup

Divide dough evenly and shape as round balls. Place on greased baking sheet(s), cover and let rise in warm place about 30 minutes. Bake in preheated 375°F (190°C) oven 15 to 20 minutes, until browned.

English Muffins

Start this early in the morning, then make the preparation a family affair in time for brunch.

	9 to 12 Muffins		12 to 18 Muffins	
All-purpose flour	500 mL	2 cups	750 mL	3 cups
Salt	5 mL	1 tsp	7 mL	1½ tsp
Sugar	2 mL	½ tsp	5 mL	1 tsp
Margarine or butter	15 mL	1 tbsp	25 mL	2 tbsp
Milk	200 mL	¾ cup	300 mL	1¼ cups
Yeast	5 mL	1 tsp	7 mL	1½ tsp
Cornmeal				

Knead dough a few times on floured surface and roll out until 1 cm (½") thick. Cut in 7 cm (3") circles. (If you do not have a cookie cutter this size, use the mouth of a drinking glass with a fine edge, dipped in flour to prevent sticking.) Place on waxed paper. Sprinkle both sides with cornmeal, if desired. Cover and let rise in warm place until doubled, about 30 minutes.

Heat cast-iron skillet or heavy griddle on medium heat 350°F (175°C). Coat with a mixture of half oil and half butter or margarine. Slip a few muffins onto skillet and fry for about 5 to 7 minutes on each side or until golden brown. Serve warm. Cooled muffins can be split and toasted.

tip

Mixing oil and butter or margarine together means a higher temperature can be reached without burning. The muffins will also absorb less fat yet have the same delicious flavour.

Pizza Pretzels

These are much like pizza in flavour, so plan on making them for a party.

	10 to 12 Pretzels		15 to 20 Pretzels	
All-purpose flour	250 mL	1 cup	375 mL	1½ cups
Whole wheat flour	250 mL	1 cup	375 mL	1½ cups
Chopped pepperoni	50 mL	¼ cup	75 mL	⅓ cup
Salt	5 mL	1 tsp	7 mL	1½ tsp
Dried oregano	2 mL	½ tsp	5 mL	1 tsp
Garlic powder	1 mL	¼ tsp	2 mL	½ tsp
Margarine or oil	15 mL	1 tbsp	25 mL	2 tbsp
Water	200 mL	¾ cup	300 mL	1¼ cups
Yeast	7 mL	1½ tsp	10 mL	2 tsp
Egg white	1	1	1	1
Water	5 mL	1 tsp	5 mL	1 tsp
Cut-up Mozzarella cheese*	250 mL	1 cup	375 mL	1½ cups

*For 250 mL (1 cup) cut-up Mozzarella cheese, you'll need 100g (3 oz). For 375 mL (1½ cups) you'll need 150g (5 oz).

Prepare dough using first group of ingredients.

Grease baking sheet(s). Cut cheese in thin pieces, small enough to fit on the narrow pretzel surface.

Knead dough a few times. Flour large chef's knife and cut dough in 10 (or 15) equal pieces. Shape each piece in log 20 cm (8") long, by rolling between floured hands or on floured surface. Twist logs in pretzel shape and place on baking sheet(s). Brush pretzels with oil. Cover and let rise in warm place until doubled in size, about 40 minutes. Brush tops of pretzels with beaten egg and water. Spread cheese over the tops.

To make pretzel shape: Make ring with dough log so ends overlap by half. Take the ends across to the opposite side of the ring, pressing overlap together.

Bake in preheated 400°F (200°C) oven for 10 to 12 minutes or until brown. Watch them: thinner pretzels cook more quickly and the cheese can make them burn easily.

Cheese Straws

These cheesy bread sticks are just right for holding appetites at bay after school.

	Sixteen 12cm (5") Sticks		Twenty-four 12cm (5") Sticks	
All-purpose flour	250 mL	1 cup	375 mL	1½ cups
Whole wheat flour	250 mL	1 cup	375 mL	1½ cups
Salt	5 mL	1 tsp	7 mL	1½ tsp
Sugar	5 mL	1 tsp	7 mL	1½ tsp
Oil	10 mL	2 tsp	15 mL	1 tbsp
Milk	200 mL	¾ cup	300 mL	1¼ cups
Yeast	10 mL	2 tsp	15 mL	1 tbsp
Grated old Cheddar cheese*	250 mL	1 cup	350 mL	1⅓ cups
Grated Parmesan cheese	25 mL	2 tbsp	35 mL	3 tbsp
Garlic salt	5 mL	1 tsp	7 mL	1½ tsp
Margarine or butter	50 mL	¼ cup	75 mL	⅓ cup

*For 250 mL (1 cup) grated Cheddar, you'll need 120 g (4 oz). For 350 mL (1⅓ cups), you'll need 170 g (6 oz).

Prepare dough using first group of ingredients.

Grease baking sheets. Mix cheeses and garlic salt in a shallow plate; set aside. Knead dough on a floured surface a few times to release air. Flour large chef's knife and cut dough in 16 (or 24) equal pieces. Shape each piece in a log 12 cm (5") long by rolling between hands or on floured surface.

Melt margarine in a glass pie plate at High power in microwave oven for 30 seconds. Roll each stick in the margarine to coat it, then roll in cheese mixture.

Place sticks on baking sheets, cover with cloth and let rise in warm place, about 15 minutes. Bake in preheated 375°F (190°C) oven for 15 to 20 minutes, until crisp and brown.

Salt Sticks

These make tantalizing tapas or cocktail party munchies.

	Thirty 7cm (3") Sticks		Fifty 7cm (3") Sticks	
All-purpose flour	500 mL	2 cups	750 mL	3 cups
Sugar	15 mL	1 tbsp	25 mL	2 tbsp
Salt	5 mL	1 tsp	7 mL	1½ tsp
Oil	15 mL	1 tbsp	25 mL	2 tbsp
Egg yolk	1	1	2	2
Water	200 mL	¾ cup	300 mL	1¼ cups
Yeast	5 mL	1 tsp	7 mL	1½ tsp
Egg white	1	1	2	2
Water	5 mL	1 tsp	10 mL	2 tsp
Coarse salt	15 mL	1 tbsp	25 mL	2 tbsp
Caraway seeds	15 mL	1 tbsp	25 mL	2 tbsp

Prepare dough using first group of ingredients.

Grease 2 to 3 baking sheets.

Knead dough a few times on a floured surface to release air. Flour large chef's knife and cut dough in 30 (or 50) equal pieces. Shape each piece in a log by rolling between floured hands or on floured surface.

Place logs on baking sheets, cover with cloth and let rise in warm place, about 15 minutes.

Brush with mixture of beaten egg white and water. Sprinkle with or roll in mixture of salt and seeds.

Bake in preheated 400°F (200°C) oven, for 10 to 12 minutes or until dry.

tip: *for large bread stick follow shaping directions for cheese straws (page 111).*

Pepper Sticks

The pepper is very hot on these sticks but they make an interesting partner with mild creamed soup.

	20 to 30 Sticks			30 to 40 Sticks		
All-purpose flour	250	mL	1 cup	375	mL	1½ cups
Rye flour	125	mL	½ cup	200	mL	¾ cup
Whole wheat flour	125	mL	½ cup	200	mL	¾ cup
Ricotta cheese	125	mL	½ cup	200	mL	¾ cup
Grated Parmesan cheese	25	mL	2 tbsp	35	mL	3 tbsp
Margarine	15	mL	1 tbsp	25	mL	2 tbsp
Water	100	mL	⅓ cup	200	mL	¾ cup
Yeast	5	mL	1 tsp	7	mL	1½ tsp
Egg	1		1	1		1
Water	15	mL	1 tbsp	15	mL	1 tbsp
Coarsely ground black pepper	10	mL	2 tsp	15	mL	1 tbsp
Crushed red pepper	10	mL	2 tsp	15	mL	1 tbsp
Poppy or sesame seeds	15	mL	1 tbsp	25	mL	2 tbsp

Prepare dough using first group of ingredients.

Grease 2 to 3 baking sheets.

Knead dough a few times on a floured surface to release air. Flour large chef's knife and cut dough in 20 to 30 (or 30 to 40) equal pieces. Shape each piece in a log by rolling between floured hands or on floured surface. Place logs on baking sheets, cover with cloth and let rise in warm place, about 15 minutes.

Brush with beaten egg and water. Sprinkle with or roll in mixture of peppers and seeds. Bake in a preheated 400°F (200°C) oven for 15 to 20 minutes or until dry.

Shape variations: Roll dough until 3 cm (⅛") thick. Cut in either of the following shapes and finish as logs above.

Twists: Cut in sticks 1 x 8 cm (⅓"x 3") long. Twist the sticks two to three times, pushing both ends down securely on the baking sheet. Yields 88 or 132 sticks.

Crackers: Cut in 3 x 5 cm (1"x 2") rectangles, place on baking sheets and finish like sticks. If you have a ripple cutter, the crackers will have an interesting appearance. Yields 68 or 100 crackers.

Bake 20 to 25 minutes or until dry.

Dough   *Yeast dough can be handled, so use the cut-up bits. Unlike pie pastry, it will not toughen.*

Pita Breads

Whole wheat pitas are very popular for sandwiches or instead of rolls with a meal. Pan-baking produces a flavour worth experiencing.

	8 Pitas		12 Pitas	
All-purpose flour	375 mL	1½ cup	500 mL	2 cups
Whole wheat flour	125 mL	½ cup	250 mL	1 cup
Salt	5 mL	1 tsp	7 mL	1½ tsp
Olive oil	15 mL	1 tbsp	25 mL	2 tbsp
Water	200 mL	¾ cup	250 mL	1 cup
Yeast	5 mL	1 tsp	7 mL	1½ tsp
Cornmeal				

Knead dough a few times on a floured surface and divide in 8 (or 12) equal pieces. Roll as balls and flatten to 1 cm (¼") rounds, using either floured hands or rolling pin. Sprinkle 2 baking sheets generously with cornmeal. Place pitas on baking sheets, cover and let rise in warm place until doubled, about 30 minutes.

To Cook:

Method 1. Bake in a preheated 500°F (240°C), oven on lowest shelf for 10 to 12 minutes or until puffed up and browned.

Method 2. Preheat heavy ungreased griddle or large frying pan on stove-top at medium-high heat. Fry 2 to 3 minutes until lightly browned. Turn once. Press surface of pitas to allow steam to spread and create air bubble inside.

Naan (Indian Flat Bread)

Every Indian meal requires naan to sop up tasty curries. Ghee or clarified butter is often used in traditional Indian cooking.

	8 Breads		12 Breads	
All-purpose or whole wheatflour	500 mL	2 cups	750 mL	3 cups
Salt	5 mL	1 tsp	7 mL	1½ tsp
Sugar	5 mL	1 tsp	7 mL	1½ tsp
Baking soda	5 mL	1 tsp	7 mL	1½ tsp
Butter, ghee or margarine	15 mL	1 tbsp	25 mL	2 tbsp
Plain yogurt	50 mL	¼ cup	125 mL	½ cup
Water	175 mL	⅔ cup	175 mL	⅔ cup
Yeast	7 mL	1½ tsp	10 mL	2 tsp
Melted butter, ghee or margarine	15 mL	1 tbsp	25 mL	2 tbsp
Sesame seeds, onion seeds or chopped onion	15 mL	1 tbsp	25 mL	2 tbsp

Prepare dough using first group of ingredients.

Knead dough a few times on a floured surface and divide into 8 (or 12) equal pieces. Roll into balls and flatten until 1 cm (¼") thick, using either floured hands or rolling pin. Place on baking sheets. Brush with melted butter, turn over and sprinkle with seeds or chopped onion.

Bake in preheated 400°F (200°C) oven for 8 to 10 minutes or until brown spots appear on top. Or fry as pitas. Serve hot. When cool, they can be wrapped in foil and reheated in a 400°F (200°C) oven about 10 minutes or individually popped into toaster.

tip: *Make pitas and naan the right size to fit your toaster.*

Limpa Rye Bread

It's a great loaf to cut in chunks, butter and enjoy with chili or stew.

	1 Loaf		2 Loaves	
All-purpose flour	375 mL	1½ cups	625 mL	2½ cups
Rye starter (see page 83)	175 mL	⅔ cup	225 mL	⅞ cup
Grated orange peel	5 mL	1 tsp	7 mL	1½ tsp
Salt	2 mL	½ tsp	5 mL	1 tsp
Fennel seed	1 mL	¼ tsp	2 mL	½ tsp
Margarine	15 mL	1 tbsp	25 mL	2 tbsp
Molasses	25 mL	2 tbsp	35 mL	3 tbsp
Water	50 mL	¼ cup	125 mL	½ cup
Yeast	7 mL	1½ tsp	10 mL	2 tsp

Knead dough a few times on floured surface. Shape as 1 (or 2) rounds and place on greased baking sheet or in round cake pan(s), which help keep the shape.

Bake in preheated 350°F (175°C) oven 20 to 30 minutes or until loaf sounds hollow when tapped on top and bottom lifts free of pan.

Pizza Dough

Pizza is always popular. For toppings use one of the variations below or your own favourite.

	one 30cm (12") round or two 20cm (8") rounds or 1 rectangular pan		two 30cm (12") rounds or three 20cm (8") rounds or 2 rectangular pans	
All-purpose flour	250 mL	1 cup	375 mL	1½ cups
Whole wheat flour	250 mL	1 cup	375 mL	1½ cups
Salt	5 mL	1 tsp	7 mL	1½ tsp
Olive oil	25 mL	2 tbsp	35 mL	3 tbsp
Water	225 mL	⅞ cup	325 mL	1¼ cups
Yeast	10 mL	2 tsp	15 mL	1 tbsp
Cornmeal (optional)				

Grease pans and sprinkle with cornmeal.

Knead risen dough on floured surface until no longer sticky. Place on pan; stretch dough with oiled fingers, being careful not to tear dough, OR roll out on pan with rolling pin, to edge of pan (dough will be springy so keep stretching until it stays in place). Spread with desired topping. Preheat oven 20 minutes before baking as a very hot oven is important.

> ### tip
> *If your bread machine holds 1 litre (4 cups) of flour, you can double the small pizza dough recipe to make three large pizzas.*

Mediterranean Topping

Lamb sausage, crumbled	250 g	½ lb	375 g	¾ lb
Yogurt	250 mL	1 cup	375 mL	1½ cups
Lemon juice	15 mL	1 tbsp	25 mL	2 tbsp
Salt	1 mL	¼ tsp	2 mL	½ tsp

Pepper	dash	dash	dash	dash
Olive oil	25 mL	2 tbsp	35 mL	3 tbsp
Slivered onion	50 mL	¼ cup	75 mL	⅓ cup
Thinly sliced green pepper	50 mL	¼ cup	75 mL	⅓ cup
Tomatoes, seeded and chopped	2	2	3	3

Fry sausage meat over medium heat for 10 minutes or until brown; let cool during dough cycle. Combine yogurt, lemon juice, salt and pepper; set aside. To assemble, spread oil on crust; spread lamb evenly on crust and sprinkle with onion, green pepper and tomatoes. Pour yogurt mixture over top.

Bake in preheated 400°F (200°C) oven for 30 to 40 minutes or until ingredients are cooked and crust browns.

Greek Topping

Olive oil	25 mL	2 tbsp	35 mL	3 tbsp
Cut-up broccoli or sliced zucchini	250 mL	1 cup	375 mL	1½ cups
Sardines (100 g)	2 cans	2 cans	3 cans	3 cans
Crumbled Feta cheese*	250 mL	1 cup	375 mL	1½ cups
Red-onion slices	5	5	8	8
Ripe olives, halved	75 mL	⅓ cup	125 mL	½ cup
Nutmeg, oregano, mint, parsley and black pepper				

*For 250 mL (1 cup) crumbled Feta cheese you'll need 200g (6 oz) and for 375 mL (1½ cups) you'll need 300g (9 oz).

To assemble, spread oil over crust. Spread evenly with broccoli, sardines, feta cheese, red-onion rings, olives and herbs.

Bake in preheated 400°F (200°C) oven for 20 to 30 minutes until crust browns.

Sausage Topping

Italian sausage, crumbled	475 g	1 lb	700 g	1½ lb
Plum tomatoes, canned	540 mL	19 oz	796 mL	28 oz
Grated mozzarella cheese	250 mL	1 cup	375 mL	1½ cups
Dried fennel	0.5 mL	⅛ tsp	1 mL	¼ tsp
Dried oregano	1 mL	¼ tsp	2 mL	½ tsp
Dried basil	5 mL	1 tsp	7 mL	1½ tsp
Salt and pepper				

Fry sausage over medium heat for 10 minutes or until brown; let cool during dough cycle. Drain and chop tomatoes.

To assemble, spread crust with sausage, cheese, tomatoes, fennel, oregano, basil, salt and pepper.

Bake in preheated 500°F (240°C) oven for 10 minutes, then reduce temperature to 400°F (200°C) for 20 to 30 minutes until crust browns.

Foldover Pizza

This tidy parcel of pizza, found in northern Italy, is ideal for lunch bags.

	three 25cm (10") rounds		five 25cm (10") rounds	
Plum tomatoes, canned	540 mL	19 oz	796 mL	28 oz
Pepperoni, sliced	300 g	½ lb	450 g	1 lb
Chopped onion	50 mL	¼ cup	75 mL	⅓ cup

Garlic powder, dried oregano, salt and pepper

Prepare rounds, 3 mm (⅛") thick. Drain and chop tomatoes. Spread tomatoes, pepperoni, onion, garlic powder, oregano, salt and pepper over half of each round, leaving border around edge. Fold dough over filling and seal edges together.

Bake in preheated 400°F (200°C) oven for 30 to 40 minutes or until browned.

Pissaladière

This popular cousin of pizza is found in southern France.

	two 25cm (10") rounds		three 25cm (10") rounds	
Olive oil	15 mL	1 tbsp	25 mL	2 tbsp
Chopped onions	2	2	3	3
Garlic clove, minced	2	2	3	3
Dried parsley	25 mL	2 tbsp	35 mL	3 tbsp
Dried thyme	1 mL	¼ tsp	2 mL	½ tsp
Bay leaf	1	1	1	1
Ground cloves, pepper	dash	dash	dash	dash
Anchovy fillets	8	8	14	14
Ripe olives, halved	16	16	30	30
Olive oil	15 mL	1 tbsp	25 mL	2 tbsp

Cook oil, onions, garlic, parsley, thyme and bay leaf in microwave oven at Medium (50%) power 4 to 5 minutes until tender. Let cool and sprinkle with dash of cloves and pepper.

To assemble, roll out rounds of dough and spread with onions. Make a pattern on top with anchovies. Place olives in between and drizzle with oil.

Bake in preheated 400°F (200°C) oven 15 to 20 minutes or until bubbling.

Variation: thinly slice 2 (or 4) plum tomatoes and arrange on Pissaladière dough first.

Focaccia

Every kitchen does something homey with leftover dough. This lightly seasoned bread round makes a fragrant snack. Garam masala can be found with the spices in the supermarket or at East Indian stores.

	three rounds		*five rounds*	
Olive oil	25 mL	2 tbsp	50 mL	¼ cup
Chopped ripe olives	8	8	14	14
Chopped pistachio nuts	50 mL	¼ cup	75 mL	⅓ cup
Garam masala	15 mL	1 tbsp	25 mL	2 tbsp
Cornmeal				

Using Pizza Dough, Plain Dough, or Low-Fat Dough, divide dough in 3 (or 5) equal parts. Roll dough out in flat rounds on floured surface or, using oiled hands, pat to 1 cm (½") thick. Place rounds on baking sheet(s) sprinkled with cornmeal. Use a chopstick or wooden spoon handle to indent dough evenly. Brush with olive oil. Sprinkle with olives, nuts and garam masala. Bake in a preheated 450°F (230°C) oven 15 to 20 minutes or until crisp.

Meat Turnovers

Make these to send to school or back to university with children and young adults. Freeze both these and the Empañadas variation for heating up later in the microwave.

	8 to 9 Turnovers		12 to 15 Turnovers	
Dough:				
All-purpose flour	500 mL	2 cups	750 mL	3 cups
Millet or corn flour	75 mL	⅓ cup	125 mL	½ cup
Sugar	10 mL	2 tsp	15 mL	1 tbsp
Salt	5 mL	1 tsp	7 mL	1½ tsp
Oil	15 mL	1 tbsp	25 mL	2 tbsp
Water	250 mL	1 cup	375 mL	1½ cups
Yeast	5 mL	1 tsp	7 mL	1½ tsp
Filling:				
Ground beef	250 g	½ lb	375 g	¾ lb
Chopped onions	35 mL	3 tbsp	50 mL	¼ cup
Cubed potatoes	250 mL	1 cup	375 mL	1½ cups
Cubed carrots	125 mL	½ cup	200 mL	¾ cup
Salt	2 mL	½ tsp	5 mL	1 tsp
Dried parsley	2 mL	½ tsp	5 mL	1 tsp
Dried basil	2 mL	½ tsp	5 mL	1 tsp
Pepper	0.5 mL	⅛ tsp	1 mL	¼ tsp
Garlic powder	0.5 mL	⅛ tsp	1 mL	¼ tsp
Nutmeg	0.5 mL	⅛ tsp	1 mL	¼ tsp
Milk				

Cook filling while dough is being made so filling will be cool enough to handle. Cook ground beef in large nonstick skillet over medium heat for 4 to 5 minutes. Stir in onions and cook until meat is no longer pink. Meanwhile, cook potatoes and carrots, with a few drops of water, in covered dish, in microwave, at High power, 4 to 5 minutes, until tender. Drain and add to skillet, along with salt, parsley, basil, pepper, garlic and nutmeg. Cook and stir a few minutes to combine flavours, then set aside to cool. Filling can be blended in food processor if a soft consistency is desired.

Grease baking sheets.

When dough is ready, knead on a floured surface, and roll out to 3 mm (⅛") thickness. Cut in 8 or 9 (12 or 15) squares or 13 cm (5") circles. Divide filling evenly among dough, placing some in centre of each. Bring edges of dough together by pinching along top to seal in filling. Place on ungreased baking sheet(s), cover and let rise in warm place for 30 minutes. Brush with milk.

Bake in preheated 375°F (190°C) oven for 30 to 40 minutes or until browned. Serve warm or cold. To freeze, let cool and wrap individually. Can be frozen for up to 3 months.

Empañadas Filling

Although the dough is not typical of Argentina, the traditional filling is appropriate and delicious.

	8 to 9 Turnovers		12 to 15 Turnovers	
Olive oil	15 mL	1 tbsp	25 mL	2 tbsp
Chopped onions	125 mL	½ cup	200 mL	¾ cup
Finely cubed beef round	250 g	½ lb	380 g	¾ lb
Chopped raisins	25 mL	2 tbsp	35 mL	3 tbsp
Hot chilies or crushed red pepper	5 mL	1 tsp	7 mL	1½ tsp
Salt	2 mL	½ tsp	5 mL	1 tsp
Paprika	2 mL	½ tsp	5 mL	1 tsp
Ground cumin	1 mL	¼ tsp	2 mL	½ tsp
Pepper				
Hard-cooked eggs cut in wedges	2	2	3	3
Pitted green olives	8 to 9	8 to 9	12 to 15	12 to 15

In a large skillet heat oil over medium heat for 2 to 3 minutes. Add onions and cook 2 to 3 minutes. Add meat, raisins and seasonings.

Cook until meat is no longer pink, about 10 minutes. Let cool. Prepare dough as for Meat Turnovers, making circles. Fill each dough circle with meat mixture. Top with some egg and an olive before sealing. Fold dough over so Empañadas resemble a crescent. Bake in preheated 375°F (190°C) for 30 to 40 minutes or until browned.

tip: *Wrap Empañadas individually for freezer storage. To heat, remove from wrap and put on plate or paper towel to thaw and heat in the microwave.*

Sesame Flour Rolls (Hua-Chan)

Make your Chinese meal more authentic with these delicacies.

	10 Rolls		15 Rolls	
Dough:				
All-purpose flour	500 mL	2 cups	750 mL	3 cups
Sugar	5 mL	1 tsp	7 mL	1½ tsp
Milk	200 mL	¾ cup	300 mL	1¼ cups
Yeast	10 mL	2 tsp	15 mL	1 tbsp
Filling:				
Sesame oil	15 mL	1 tbsp	25 mL	2 tbsp
Honey	10 mL	2 tsp	15 mL	1 tbsp
Sea salt or salt	5 mL	1 tsp	7 mL	1½ tsp
Sesame seeds, toasted	50 mL	¼ cup	75 mL	⅓ cup

Knead dough to expel air. If making large recipe, divide dough and filling in two.

Roll out dough in rectangle twice as long as wide 5 mm (¼") thick. Combine oil, honey and salt and brush over dough. Roll up dough jelly roll style, starting from wide side. Cut off pieces 2 cm (¾") long. Press floured chopstick or wooden spoon handle onto centre of each piece so that cut surfaces lift and touch and it resembles a flower. Pinch to help preserve shape. Place rolls on steaming plates or baking sheet, sprinkle on sesame seeds, cover and let rise in warm place for 30 minutes. Use a large saucepan about 3 litre (12 cups). Add water until 5 cm (2") deep and flat steaming rack or substitute tuna cans with both ends removed. Bring water to a boil. Put each roll on a small piece of waxed paper. Fit several rolls on bamboo steam tray or small plate.

Place plate(s) on steaming rack over simmering water; cook about 10 minutes or until buns are no longer sticky.

ALL-PURPOSE DOUGHS

Use the following Mix-and-Match plain doughs to make rolls, buns, filled braids and breads. Fill with the suggested Mix-and-Match fillings or any from the previous recipes. Even the pizza topping can be used as a filling.

Mix-and-Match Plain Dough

Use for filled braids, rolls and swirled rolls.

	Small		Large	
All-purpose flour	500 mL	2 cups	750 mL	3 cups
Salt	5 mL	1 tsp	7 mL	1½ tsp
Sugar	5 mL	1 tsp	7 mL	1½ tsp
Margarine	25 mL	2 tbsp	35 mL	3 tbsp
Egg plus	1	1	1	1
Water to equal	200 mL	¾ cup	300 mL	1¼ cups
Yeast	10 mL	2 tsp	15 mL	1 tbsp

Mix-and-Match Low-Fat Plain Dough

Use for filled braids, rolls and swirled rolls that have dry fillings such as Greek Pizza topping or Tomato Roll.

	Small		Large	
All-purpose flour	500 mL	2 cups	750 mL	3 cups
Salt	5 mL	1 tsp	7 mL	1½ tsp
Sugar	5 mL	1 tsp	7 mL	1½ tsp
Oil	10 mL	2 tsp	15 mL	1 tbsp
Water	200 mL	¾ cup	300 mL	1¼ cups
Yeast	7 mL	1½ tsp	10 mL	2 tsp

Mix-and-Match Whole Wheat Plain Dough

The wheat bran in the flour bakes to a nutty flavour which complements Swiss Mushroom or Spicy Cheese filling.

	Small		Large	
Whole wheat flour	500 mL	2 cups	750 mL	3 cups
Salt	5 mL	1 tsp	7 mL	1½ tsp
Sugar	5 mL	1 tsp	7 mL	1½ tsp
Margarine or oil	25 mL	2 tbsp	35 mL	3 tbsp
Egg plus	1	1	1	1
Milk or water to equal	200 mL	¾ cup	300 mL	1¼ cups
Yeast	5 mL	1 tsp	7 mL	1½ tsp

tip: *To add interest to plain doughs try these ideas:*

1. Add dried thyme	1 mL	¼ tsp	2 mL	½ tsp
2. Add dried pepper	0.5 mL	⅛ tsp	1 mL	¼ tsp
3. Add chopped fresh parsley	15 mL	1 tbsp	25 mL	2 tbsp
4. Add dried parsley	5 mL	1 tsp	7 mL	1½ tsp
5. Add garam masala	7 mL	1½ tsp	10 mL	2 tsp

Salmon Braid

For a special lunch dish, serve with a cream, mustard or velouté sauce.

	1 Loaf		2 Loaves	
1 recipe Mix-and-Match Plain Dough (white, low-fat or whole wheat)				
Filling:				
Sliced fresh mushrooms	250 mL	1 cup	375 mL	1½ cups
Salmon, canned (215 g)	1 can	1 cans	2 cans	2 cans
Fresh dill	15 mL	1 tbsp	25 mL	2 tbsp
Chopped onions	50 mL	¼ cup	75 mL	⅓ cup
Chopped green pepper	50 mL	¼ cup	75 mL	⅓ cup
Shredded Havarti cheese*	250 mL	1 cup	375 mL	1½ cups
Freshly grated pepper				

*For 250 mL (1 cup) shredded Havarti cheese, you'll need 125 g (4 oz) and for 375 mL (1½ cups) you'll need 200 g (6 oz).

If making large recipe, divide ingredients in half to prepare 2 braids. Grease baking sheet(s).

Knead dough on floured surface. On large sheet of waxed paper sprinkled with flour, roll out dough to rectangle approximately 30 x 40 cm (12 x 15"). In centre third, layer mushrooms, drained salmon, dill, onions, green pepper, Havarti and pepper. Using floured knife, cut strips 2 cm (¾") wide from edge of dough in toward filling, stopping at the "third" mark. Diagonally fold strips over filling, alternating from left and right sides. Seal dough at each end to hold in filling. Carefully slide braid(s) onto baking sheet. (You may need to reshape it at this stage. Make sure there are no thin areas.) Cover and let rise in warm place, about 20 minutes.

Bake in preheated 375°F (190°C) oven for 30 to 40 minutes or until lightly browned. Slice and serve hot.

Spicy Cheddar Swirled Rolls

When you are looking for a substantial snack-on-the-run or a satisfying brunch, this is the answer.

	10 Rolls		16 Rolls	
1 recipe Mix-and-Match Plain Dough (white, low-fat or whole wheat)				
Filling:				
Grated Cheddar cheese*	750 mL	3 cups	1.25 L	5 cups
Grated Parmesan cheese	50 mL	¼ cup	75 mL	⅓ cup
Sugar	5 mL	1 tsp	7 mL	1½ tsp
Dried Tarragon	2 mL	½ tsp	5 mL	1 tsp
Garlic powder	1 mL	¼ tsp	2 mL	½ tsp

*For 750 mL (3 cups) grated Cheddar cheese, you'll need 250 g (8 oz) and for 1.25 L (5 cups) you'll need 375 g (12 oz).

If making large recipe, divide ingredients in half to make handling easier.

Grease large baking sheet. Combine cheeses, sugar, tarragon and garlic powder.

Knead dough on floured surface. Roll out to a rectangle 5 mm (¼") thick. Spread with cheese mixture, leaving border of dough around edge. Roll up dough from the wide side and seal edge. With floured knife, cut in 10 equal pieces. Place on baking sheet, cover and let rise in warm place until doubled in size, about 30 minutes.

Bake in preheated 375°F (190°C) oven for 30 to 35 minutes or until browned. Serve warm.

tip: *Spicy Cheddar Swirled Rolls can be made in a braid shape, following directions for Salmon Braid.*

Dill Roll

When dill is in season, enjoy this as a luncheon main course accompanied by a chef's salad.

	1 Loaf			2 Loaves		
1 recipe Mix-and-Match Plain Dough (white, low-fat or whole wheat)						
Filling:						
Ricotta or dry cottage cheese	250	mL	1 cup	375	mL	1½ cups
Fresh chopped dill or	15	mL	1 tbsp	25	mL	2 tbsp
dried dill	5	mL	1 tsp	10	mL	2 tsp
Egg yolk	1		1	2		2
Pepper	1	mL	¼ tsp	2	mL	½ tsp
Oil						

If making large recipe, divide ingredients in half to make 2 loaves.

Grease loaf pan(s).

Knead dough on floured surface. Roll dough out in rectangle with the narrow side slightly wider than length of pan.

Combine cheese, dill, egg yolk and pepper. Spread cheese mixture on dough, leaving border of dough around edge. Roll up dough, seal edges and place in pan, seam-side down. Brush with oil. Cover and let rise in warm place until doubled in size, about 30 minutes.

Bake in preheated 375°F (190°C) oven for 30 to 40 minutes until lightly browned. Remove from pan to cool. Serve sliced.

Tomato Roll

An excellent appetizer to serve with red wine and seasoned olives.

	1 Loaf		2 Loaves	
1 recipe Mix-and-Match Low-Fat Plain Dough				
Filling:				
Sun-dried tomatoes, packed in oil	50 mL	¼ cup	75 mL	⅓ cup
Grated lemon peel	10 mL	2 tsp	15 mL	1 tbsp
Crushed red pepper	1	1	2	2
Garlic clove, minced	1	1	2	2
Dried thyme	5 mL	1 tsp	7 mL	1½ tbsp
Dried basil	5 mL	1 tsp	7 mL	1½ tbsp
Chopped ripe olives	8	8	14	14
Olive oil	15 mL	1 tbsp	25 mL	2 tbsp

If making large recipe, divide ingredients in half to make 2 loaves.

Grease loaf pan(s).

Combine tomatoes, olives, lemon peel, red pepper, garlic, thyme and basil.

Knead dough on floured surface. Roll dough out in a rectangle with narrow side slightly wider than length of pan. Brush oil over dough. Spread tomato mixture over dough, leaving border of dough around edge. Roll up dough, seal edges and place in pan, seam-side down. Cover and let rise in warm place until doubled in size, about 30 minutes.

Bake in preheated 375°F (190°C) oven for 30 to 40 minutes until lightly browned. Turn out of pan to cool. Serve sliced.

MIX-AND-MATCH FILLINGS

Use the following filling or those given in the previous recipes to fill buns, swirled rolls or rolled, filled bread. The Mix-and-Match Plain Doughs are perfect for this, but don't be afraid to experiment with other doughs, too.

Swiss Mushroom Filling

	Small		Large	
Flour	15 mL	1 tbsp	25 mL	2 tbsp
Margarine or butter	15 mL	1 tbsp	25 mL	2 tbsp
Milk	200 mL	¾ cup	300 mL	1¼ cups
Thinly sliced mushrooms	12 to15	12 to15	18 to 20	18 to 20
Grated Swiss cheese*	500 mL	2 cups	750 mL	3 cups
Dried tarragon	1 mL	¼ tsp	2 mL	½ tsp
Salt and pepper				

*For 500 mL (2 cups) grated Swiss cheese, you'll need 250 g (8 oz) and for 750 mL (3 cups) you'll need 375 g (12 oz).

In large microwaveable bowl, heat flour and butter together at Medium (50%) power 1 minute. Stir well, then gradually blend in milk. Heat at High power 1 minute, then Medium power 3 to 4 minutes, stirring twice until smooth and thick. Stir in mushrooms, cheese, tarragon, dash of salt and pepper.

Thoroughly combine and use as filling.

SWEET RECIPES

Two versions of sweet dough can be used for a variety of treats. Use the shapes on page 103 alone to accompany a dessert of fruit or complement a brunch buffet. Fill any shapes such as the swirled buns or make a rolled loaf with fruit suggested on page 142. Take as a hostess gift or serve at a picnic. You can mix and match the doughs, fillings, glazes and icings to create your own inspired sweet.

Mix-and-Match Sweet Dough

All-purpose flour	500	mL	2	cups	750 mL	3 cups
Sugar	50	mL	¼	cup	75 mL	⅓ cup
Margarine	25	mL	2	tbsp	35 mL	3 tbsp
Grated orange or lemon peel (optional)	5 to 10	mL	1 to 2	tsp	10 to 15 mL	2 to 3 tsp
Salt	5	mL	1	tsp	7 mL	1½ tsp
Egg plus	1		1		1	1
Milk to equal	225	mL	¾	cup	350 mL	1⅓ cups
Yeast	7	mL	1½	tsp	10 mL	2 tsp

Mix-and-Match Whole Wheat Sweet Dough

Whole wheat flour	375	mL	1½	cups	500 mL	2 cups
All-purpose flour	125	mL	½	cup	250 mL	1 cup
Sugar	25	mL	2	tbsp	50 mL	¼ cup
Brown sugar	15	mL	1	tbsp	25 mL	2 tbsp
Grated orange peel	5	mL	1	tsp	7 mL	1½ tsp
Salt	5	mL	1	tsp	7 mL	1½ tsp
Margarine or butter	25	mL	2	tbsp	50 mL	¼ cup
Egg plus	1		1		1	1
Water to equal	175	mL	⅔	cup	250 mL	1 cup
Yeast	7	mL	1½	tsp	10 mL	2 tsp

MIX-AND-MATCH SWEET FILLINGS

Anise Cheese Filling

Dry cottage cheese or ricotta cheese	250 mL	1 cup	375 mL	1½ cups
Grated orange peel	5 mL	1 tsp	7 mL	1½ tsp
Anise seeds	2 mL	½ tsp	3 mL	¾ tsp
Egg yolk	1	1	1	1

Combine cheese, orange peel, anise and egg yolk in bowl before using.

Cream Cheese Filling

Cream cheese*	250 mL	1 cup	350 mL	1¼ cups
Icing sugar	75 mL	⅓ cup	125 mL	½ cup
Currants	50 mL	¼ cup	75 mL	⅓ cup
Grated lemon peel	5 mL	1 tsp	7 mL	1½ tsp
Vanilla	2 mL	½ tsp	5 mL	1 tsp

*For 250 mL (1 cup) cream cheese, you'll need 175 g (6 oz) and for 350 mL (1¼ cups) you'll need 250 g (8 oz).

Combine cheese, icing sugar, currants, lemon peel and vanilla in bowl before using.

Date Filling

Chopped, dried dates	325 mL	1¼ cups	500 mL	2 cups
Water	175 mL	⅔ cup	250 mL	1 cup
Lemon juice	15 mL	1 tbsp	25 mL	2 tbsp

Cook dates, water and lemon juice in 1 L (4 cup) microwaveable bowl on High power for 3 to 4 minutes OR in covered saucepan over low heat, until thick and smooth, stirring several times. Cool before using.

Nut Filling

Ground almonds, hazelnuts or walnuts	250 mL	1 cup	375 mL	1½ cups
Brown sugar	50 mL	¼ cup	75 mL	⅓ cup
Soft butter or margarine	50 mL	¼ cup	75 mL	⅓ cup
Grated lemon or orange peel	10 mL	2 tsp	15 mL	1 tbsp
Vanilla or almond extract	5 mL	1 tsp	7 mL	1½ tsp

Combine nuts, brown sugar, butter, lemon peel and vanilla in bowl before using.

Poppy Seed Filling

Ground poppy seed	250 mL	1 cup	375 mL	1½ cups
Sugar	200 mL	¾ cup	300 mL	1¼ cups
Raisins	125 mL	½ cup	200 mL	¾ cup
Milk	125 mL	½ cup	200 mL	¾ cup
Grated lemon peel	10 mL	2 tsp	15 mL	1 tbsp

Combine poppy seed sugar, raisins, milk and lemon peel in a saucepan. Cover and cook over low heat in covered saucepan, stirring constantly, until spreading consistency. Cool before using.

Streusel Filling (or Topping)

Use as topping on coffee cake, rolled in swirled buns or as filling for rolled loaves.

All-purpose or whole wheat flour	125 mL	½ cup	200 mL	¾ cup
Brown sugar	125 mL	½ cup	200 mL	¾ cup
Chopped nuts	125 mL	½ cup	200 mL	¾ cup
Soft margarine or butter	50 mL	¼ cup	75 mL	⅓ cup
Cinnamon	5 mL	1 tsp	7 mL	1½ tsp

Mix flour, brown sugar, nuts, butter and cinnamon in bowl with fork.

MIX-AND-MATCH ICINGS

Most yeast rolls and cakes are even better with thin icings that are drizzled over the surface and run down the sides like icicles off a roof. Use icing on swirled buns and coffee cake.

Beat ingredients together, in a small bowl. It may be necessary to adjust the amount of liquid by adding more than recommended.

Orange Icing

	Small		Large	
Icing sugar	250 mL	1 cup	375 mL	1½ cups
Butter or margarine	25 mL	2 tbsp	50 mL	¼ cup
Orange juice	35 mL	3 tsp	50 mL	¼ cup

Combine.

Runny Lemon Icing

	Small		Large	
Icing sugar	250 mL	1 cup	375 mL	1½ cups
Water	25 mL	2 tbsp	35 mL	3 tbsp
Lemon juice	5 mL	1 tsp	10 mL	2 tsp

Combine.

Coffee Icing

	Small		Large	
Icing sugar	250 mL	1 cup	375 mL	1½ cups
Butter or margarine	15 mL	1 tbsp	25 mL	2 tbsp
Instant coffee granules	10 mL	2 tsp	15 mL	1 tbsp
Milk or water	25 mL	2 tbsp	35 mL	3 tbsp

Combine.

Vanilla Icing

	Small		Large	
Icing sugar	250 mL	1 cup	375 mL	1½ cups
Milk	25 mL	2 tbsp	35 mL	3 tbsp
Vanilla	5 mL	1 tsp	10 mL	2 tbsp

Combine.

WASHES

Applied before baking, washes or glazes (usually made with egg) add a shiny finish, browner crust and richness to whatever you bake.

Whole Egg Wash

Beat egg and brush on evenly with pastry brush. If you are a bit short of egg, add 5 mL (1 tsp) water or milk.

   This wash is very useful when sprinkling seeds on breads to hold them in place.

Egg Yolk Wash

This works much like the whole egg, but 1 yolk is beaten with 5 mL (1 tsp) water.

---

tip

Egg White Wash   *For a very shiny crust, beat 1 egg white with 5 mL (1 tsp) water until very runny. Brush evenly over surface and wipe any excess off pan or it might burn the undercrust or surface of pan.*

Milk

For a browner crust, simply brush whole milk on the surface. Using water as a wash will make the crust crisp, without changing the colour.

Shortening

Brushing melted butter, margarine, shortening or oil on shapes before rising helps keep the surface of the dough from drying, thus letting it stretch during rising. You can never go wrong if you do this every time you make hand-shaped rolls or buns. For a soft crust, brush loaves with shortening after baking.

Filled Rolled Loaves

These satisfy a sweet tooth, yet take only minutes to prepare. Use one of the suggested fillings such as Anise as a coffee break loaf.

1 recipe Mix-and-Match Sweet Dough (page 136)
1 recipe of the filling of your choice (pages 137 to 139)
1 egg wash (page 141)

If making large recipe, divide Sweet Dough and filling in two to make handling easier.

Grease baking sheets.

Knead dough a few times on floured surface.

For long, thin loaf, roll dough in a rectangle 6 mm (¼") thick. Spread filling over dough, close to narrow edge. Roll up along wide edge like a jelly roll and pinch seam closed. Place on baking sheet.

Or, for loaf pan shape, roll dough 1 cm (½") thick. Spread on filling in a rectangle and roll up along narrow edge and pinch seams closed. Placed seamside down in greased loaf pan(s).

Brush with some of egg wash, cover and let rise in warm place until doubled in size, about 30 minutes. Brush with remaining egg wash.

Bake in preheated 350°F (175°C) oven for 35 to 45 minutes or until browned.

Hungarian Christmas Bread

It's traditional for Hungarian families to serve this thinly sliced along with coffee for Yuletide visitors.

1 recipe Mix-and-Match Sweet Dough
1 recipe Poppy Seed Filling (page 138)
1 egg wash

If making large recipe, divide dough and filling in two to make handling easier.

Grease baking sheet.

Knead dough a few times on floured surface, then roll dough into rectangle 6 mm (¼") thick. Spread filling over dough, close to narrow edge. Roll up along narrow edge like a jelly roll and pinch seam closed. Place on baking sheet. Brush with some egg wash, cover and let rise in warm place until doubled in size, about 30 minutes. Brush with remaining egg.

Bake in preheated 350°F (175°C) oven for 40 to 50 minutes or until lightly browned. Remove from pan to cool. Will keep for several weeks in cold place if well wrapped.

Rhubarb Kuchen

The tart yet sweet flavour of this cake is a treat for rhubarb lovers.

	2 square cake pans or 1 oblong cake pan		3 square cake pans	
1 recipe Mix-and-Match Sweet Dough (page 136)				
Topping:				
Sliced rhubarb	750 mL	3 cups	1 mL	4 cups
Sugar	175 mL	⅔ cup	250 mL	1 cup
Cinnamon	5 mL	1 tsp	7 mL	1½ tsp
Egg yolk	1	1	2	2
Milk	25 mL	2 tbsp	35 mL	3 tbsp

Combine rhubarb, sugar, cinnamon, egg yolk and milk in bowl while dough is rising. Grease pans.

Divide dough in 2 (or 3) equal portions and spread each evenly in pan, using fingers to smooth in corners. Divide rhubarb mixture in 2 (or 3) and spoon over top. Cover and let rise in a warm place until doubled, about 30 minutes.

Bake in preheated 400°F (200°C) oven 30 to 35 minutes or until top is browned. Cut in squares and serve warm or cold.

Seasonal Coffee Cake

Serve with evening coffee for a hit with family and friends. Depending on what fruit is in season, choose peaches, apples or blueberries.

	2 square cake pans or 1 oblong cake pan		3 square cake pans	
1 Recipe Mix-and-Match Sweet Dough				
Sliced fruit	750 mL	3 cups	1 mL	4 cups
Brown sugar	200 mL	¾ cup	300 mL	1¼ cups
Lemon juice	15 mL	1 tbsp	25 mL	2 tbsp
Cinnamon	5 mL	1 tsp	7 mL	1½ tsp
Vanilla or almond extract	5 mL	1 tsp	7 mL	1½ tsp

Combine sliced fruit, brown sugar, lemon juice, cinnamon and vanilla in bowl. Grease pans.

Divide Sweet Dough and spread in pans, using floured hands. Top with fruit mixture. Cover and let rise in a warm place until doubled, about 30 minutes.

Bake in preheated 400°F (200°C) oven 30 to 35 minutes or until top is browned. Cut in squares and serve warm or cold.

Hungarian Coffee Cake

Sometimes called bubble bread, the sweet sticky cake can be pulled apart with fingers to enjoy.

	2L (8")tube pan or 1 loaf pan		*4L (10") tube pan or 2 loaf pans*	
1 recipe Mix-and-Match Sweet Dough				
Chopped nuts	50 mL	¼ cup	75 mL	⅓ cup
Raisins	50 mL	¼ cup	75 mL	⅓ cup
Chopped maraschino cherries	25 mL	2 tbsp	35 mL	3 tbsp
Butter	50 mL	¼ cup	75 mL	⅓ cup
Sugar	100 mL	⅓ cup	125 mL	½ cup
Brown sugar	50 mL	¼ cup	75 mL	⅓ cup
Cinnamon	10 mL	2 tsp	15 mL	1 tbsp

Grease pan. Combine nuts, raisins and cherries in small bowl. Melt butter in another small bowl in microwave at Medium (50%) power, covered with waxed paper (20 to 40 seconds). Combine sugar, brown sugar and cinnamon in bowl.

On floured surface, shape Sweet Dough into 4 cm (1½") round balls. Dip balls into melted butter, then into cherry mixture. Layer balls in pan, sprinkling some cinnamon mixture and cherry mixture over each layer. If there is any butter or cinnamon mixture left, spread over top. Cover and let rise in warm place until doubled, about 30 minutes.

Bake in preheated 375°F (190°C) oven for 30 to 40 minutes or until browned on top.

Scandinavian Coffee Cake

This spectacular ring makes a perfect hostess gift that you will always be remembered for. Use 3-fruit marmalade, apricot or raspberry jam and walnuts for a memorable taste.

	1 Ring		*2 Rings*	
1 recipe Mix-and-Match Sweet Dough (page 136)				
Filling:				
Jam or marmalade	125 mL	½ cup	200 mL	¾ cup
Raisins or chopped nuts	50 mL	¼ cup	75 mL	⅓ cup
Cinnamon	5 mL	1 tsp	7 mL	1½ tsp

1 egg wash (page 141)

Icing of your choice (page 140), if desired.

If making large recipe, divide dough and filling ingredients in half.

Grease baking sheet(s).

Roll dough out on floured surface to rectangle about 6 mm (¼") thick. Spread jam over dough close to the edge. Sprinkle with raisins or nuts and cinnamon. Roll up dough along the wide edge and seal by pinching seam together with fingers. Lift onto baking sheet and shape in a ring, pinching together the part where the two ends meet. Carefully, with a sharp knife, cut about three-quarters of the way through ring toward centre, beginning at outside edge, spacing cuts evenly about 2 cm (¾") apart. Turn each piece slightly, so that cut side shows filling. Cover and let rise in warm place until doubled, about 30 minutes.

Brush with egg wash and bake in preheated 375°F (190°C) oven for 35 to 45 minutes or until lightly browned.

Drizzle with icing and sprinkle with additional chopped nuts, if desired. Serve in slices.

tip: *Any of the suggested fillings on pages 137 to 138 are suitable for this shape, which always looks spectacular. A popular treatment for a Christmas theme is red and green glacéed cherries or candied peel in the filling and on top.*

Chocolate Monkey Bread

Although the origin of the name is a mystery to me, it's another fun pull-apart sweet bread.

	2L (8")tube or 2 loaf pans		4L (10") tube or 3 loaf pans	
Dough:				
All-purpose flour	500 mL	2 cups	750 mL	3 cups
Sugar	50 mL	¼ cup	75 mL	⅓ cup
Butter or margarine	25 mL	2 tbsp	35 mL	3 tbsp
Salt	5 mL	1 tsp	7 mL	1½ tsp
Grated orange rind	5 mL	1 tsp	7 mL	1½ tsp
Egg	1	1	1	1
Milk	175 mL	⅔ cup	250 mL	1 cup
Yeast	7 mL	1½ tsp	10 mL	2 tsp
Dippings:				
Butter or margarine	50 mL	¼ cup	75 mL	⅓ cup
Sugar	125 mL	½ cup	225 mL	¾ cup
Ground pecans	25 mL	2 tbsp	35 mL	3 tbsp
Cocoa	15 mL	1 tbsp	25 mL	2 tbsp
Cinnamon	7 mL	1½ tsp	10 mL	2 tsp

Prepare dough. Grease pan. Melt butter in small bowl in microwave at Medium power (50%), covered with waxed paper 20 to 40 seconds. Mix sugar, pecans, cocoa and cinnamon in another small bowl.

Knead dough with floured hands to remove air bubbles. Shape in 3 cm (1") balls. Line up bowls of butter and sugar mixture and pan. Dip each ball into butter, then sugar mixture, then layer evenly in pan. If any butter or sugar mixture remain, pour over the top. Cover pan with towel and let rise in warm place until doubled, about 20 minutes.

Bake in a preheated 350°F (175°C) oven for 35 to 45 minutes.

Let cool about 15 minutes, then invert onto serving plate. Pieces are usually pulled apart but loaf can be sliced.

Sour Cream Coffee Rolls

During the winter, yeast buns are welcome as a dessert or snack. These are very light.

	8 to 10 Rolls		10 to 15 Rolls	
Dough:				
All-purpose flour	500 mL	2 cups	750 mL	3 cups
Sugar	15 mL	1 tbsp	25 mL	2 tbsp
Salt	5 mL	1 tsp	7 mL	1½ tsp
Sour cream	35 mL	3 tbsp	50 mL	¼ cup
Margarine or butter	15 mL	1 tbsp	25 mL	2 tbsp
Egg	1	1	1	1
Milk	50 mL	¼ cup	125 mL	½ cup
Yeast	7 mL	1½ tsp	10 mL	2 tsp
Filling:				
Chopped, dried, pitted prunes	125 mL	½ cup	200 mL	¾ cup
Chopped walnuts	50 mL	¼ cup	75 mL	⅓ cup
Sugar	35 mL	3 tbsp	50 mL	¼ cup
Cinnamon	1 mL	¼ tsp	2 mL	½ tsp

Prepare dough. If making large recipe, divide Dough and Filling ingredients in half.

Grease 1 or 2 cake pans. Combine prunes, nuts, sugar and cinnamon. Knead dough on floured surface a few times. Using floured rolling pin, roll dough in a rectangle 3 cm (⅛") thick. Sprinkle with filling, leaving edges free for sealing. Roll up along narrow edge and pinch seam closed. With floured knife, cut in 8 to 10 (or 10 to 15) slices and put in pan(s) cut side down and evenly spaced. Cover with towel and let rise in warm place until doubled, about 30 minutes. Bake preheated in 375°F (190°C) oven for 20 to 30 minutes or until browned. To serve, invert the rolls.

Breakfast Bagels

These sweetish bagels will give pleasure to the aficionados, even Montrealers.

	10 to 12 Bagels		16 to 18 Bagels	
All-purpose flour	500 mL	2 cups	750 mL	3 cups
Salt	7 mL	1½ tsp	10 mL	2 tsp
Oil	15 mL	1 tbsp	25 mL	2 tbsp
Honey	50 mL	¼ cup	75 mL	⅓ cup
Egg yolk	1	1	2	2
Water	150 mL	½ cup	225 mL	⅞ cup
Yeast	10 mL	2 tsp	15 mL	1 tbsp
Water	1.5 L	6 cups	1.5 L	6 cups
Honey	25 mL	2 tbsp	25 mL	2 tbsp
Egg or egg white	1	1	1	1
Water	5 mL	1 tsp	5 mL	1 tsp

Sesame seeds, poppy seeds,
diced onion, or coarse (kosher) salt

Cornmeal

Prepare dough using first group of ingredients.

Meanwhile, line 2 baking sheets with waxed paper for the rising. Grease baking sheets or line with parchment baking paper; sprinkle with cornmeal for the baking.

On floured board or sheet of waxed paper, divide dough in 10 (or 16) equal pieces. Roll each piece between hands and push a hole through centre with fingers. Stretch hole to about 5 cm (2") diameter by pulling evenly around in circle. Tradition does not allow using a doughnut cutter.

Cover bagels with towel and put in warm place to rise until almost doubled in size, about 20 to 30 minutes. Meanwhile bring water and honey to boil in a large 5 L (20 cup) pot. Place about 3 or 4 bagels in boiling water at a time. Regulate the heat so water stays simmering. Bagels will sink. Once they rise, boil for 1 minute, turn over and cook for 1 minute. Remove bagels and place on greased baking sheet(s).

Beat egg white and water and brush over bagels. Sprinkle tops with seeds, diced onions or salt.

Bake in preheated 400°F (200°C) oven for 25 to 30 minutes or until brown. Bagels should rise some more during baking. Enjoy warm or cold, sliced and toasted or reheated.

To reheat: Place on paper towel and heat in microwave at Medium (50%) power for 40 to 60 seconds. The centre will heat faster than the outside. Don't overheat; if you heat them until hot to the touch, they will become tough.

Variations: Cinnamon Bagels – add 10 mL (2 tsp) cinnamon for small and 15 mL (3 tbsp) for large dough recipe.

Kugelhopf

This old-world German favourite looks wonderful made in a Kugelhopf pan. A Bundt pan holds the modern version. The flavour hints of lemon and almonds.

	2 L (8") tube pan Kugelhopf or Bundt pan		4 L (10") tube pan Kugelhopf or Bundt pan	
All-purpose flour	500 mL	2 cups	750 mL	3 cups
Raisins	125 mL	½ cup	200 mL	¾ cup
Sugar	75 mL	⅓ cup	125 mL	½ cup
Ground almonds	75 mL	⅓ cup	125 mL	½ cup
Salt	5 mL	1 tsp	7 mL	1½ tsp
Grated lemon peel	5 mL	1 tsp	7 mL	1½ tsp
Butter or margarine	75 mL	⅓ cup	125 mL	½ cup
Egg	1	1	1	1
plus milk to equal	225 mL	⅞ cup	350 mL	1⅓ cups
Yeast	7 mL	1½ tsp	10 mL	2 tsp

Grease pan. Put dough into pan, stretching and patting to fit properly. Cover with towel and let rise in warm place until doubled, about 20 minutes. Bake in preheated 350°F (180°C) oven 30 to 40 minutes or until browned. Let cool in pan for about 15 minutes, then invert onto serving plate. Ice with thin (page 140) drizzled down the sides, if desired.

Special Cake Dough

It's the delicious beginning for making Savarin Cake and Baba au Rhum.

	Small		Large	
All-purpose flour	500 mL	2 cups	750 mL	3 cups
Sugar	25 mL	2 tbsp	35 mL	3 tbsp
Salt	2 mL	½ tsp	5 mL	1 tsp
Butter or margarine	75 mL	⅓ cup	125 mL	½ cup
Eggs	2	2	3	3
Milk	125 mL	½ cup	200 mL	¾ cup
Yeast	7 mL	1½ tsp	10 mL	2 tsp

Savarin Cake

This cake looks very elegant piped with cream and garnished with mandarin orange segments and candied violets.

	2 L (8") tube pan or Savarin pan*		4 L (10") tube pan or Savarin pan*	
1 Recipe Special Cake Dough (page 153)				
Syrup:				
Sugar	250 mL	1 cup	375 mL	1½ cups
Orange juice	175 mL	⅔ cup	250 mL	1 cup
Water	175 mL	⅔ cup	250 mL	1 cup
Brandy (optional)	25 mL	2 tbsp	35 mL	3 tbsp
Glaze:				
Orange marmalade	50 mL	¼ cup	75 mL	⅓ cup
Water	15 mL	1 tbsp	25 mL	2 tbsp
Garnish:				
Whipped cream	250 mL	1 cup	375 mL	1½ cups
Mandarin orange segments	9	9	15	15
Candied violets (optional)				

Put Special Cake Dough in greased pan. Cover with towel and let rise in a warm place until doubled, about 40 minutes. Bake in preheated 400°F (200°C) oven for 35 to 40 minutes or until browned.

Meanwhile, prepare syrup by boiling sugar, orange juice and water on stovetop for 5 minutes or in microwave at High power for 30 to 40 seconds. Stir in brandy.

Invert cake onto serving plate. Prick surface of cake with long-tined fork or skewer and spoon syrup over cake until absorbed. When cake has cooled, spread glaze evenly over it. Just before serving, pipe dollops of cream decoratively around base of cake and garnish with orange segments. Refrigerate.

*Savarin pans are similar to ring gelatin moulds yet lower than tube pans.

Baba Au Rhum

Luscious is the only word to describe this rum-flavoured treat.

1 recipe Special Cake Dough (page 153)	2 L (8") tube pan		4 L (10") tube pan	
Filling:				
Raisins	50 mL	¼ cup	75 mL	⅓ cup
Currants	50 mL	¼ cup	75 mL	⅓ cup
Syrup:				
Sugar	250 mL	1 cup	375 mL	1½ cups
Water	250 mL	1 cup	375 mL	1½ cups
Rum or rum flavouring	25 mL	2 tbsp	35 mL	3 tbsp

Put half of Special Cake Dough in greased tube pan. Sprinkle with raisins and currants, then top with remaining dough. Cover with towel and let rise in a warm place until doubled, about 40 minutes.

Bake in preheated 400°F (200°C) oven for 25 to 35 minutes or until browned. Let cool on rack.

Meanwhile, boil sugar and water on stove-top for 5 minutes or microwave at Medium power for 3 to 4 minutes, then stir in rum. Invert cake onto serving plate. Gradually pour syrup over cake, basting cake with syrup from plate until most of it is absorbed. This should take 15 minutes. Cool before cutting.

Individual Babas

To make individual babas prepare as above (small recipe converts to 12 baba moulds and the large recipe converts to 18 baba moulds), let rise and bake for 20 to 30 minutes. Complete as above.

Cinnamon Crisps

The extra effort required to make these cookies is well worth the reward. They are just as crispy and cinnamony as can be.

	14 Crisps		21 Crisps	
Dough:				
All-purpose flour	500 mL	2 cups	750 mL	3 cups
Sugar	25 mL	2 tbsp	35 mL	3 tbsp
Salt	2 mL	½ tsp	5 mL	1 tsp
Butter or margarine	25 mL	2 tbsp	35 mL	3 tbsp
Eggs	1	1	2	2
Milk	175 mL	⅔ cup	250 mL	1 cup
Yeast	5 mL	1 tsp	7 mL	1½ tsp
Filling:				
Butter or margarine	25 mL	2 tbsp	35 mL	3 tbsp
Sugar	50 mL	¼ cup	75 mL	⅓ cup
Brown sugar	50 mL	¼ cup	75 mL	⅓ cup
Cinnamon	1 mL	¼ tsp	2 mL	½ tsp
Topping:				
Butter or margarine, melted	25 mL	2 tbsp	35 mL	3 tbsp
Sugar	125 mL	½ cup	200 mL	¾ cup
Chopped pecans	50 mL	¼ cup	75 mL	⅓ cup
Cinnamon	2 mL	½ tsp	5 mL	1 tsp

Prepare dough and turn out on a floured surface, kneading a few times. Roll out to 30 cm (12") square for small recipe (45 x 30 cm (18"x 12") rectangle for large recipe. Prepare filling in a large bowl. Melt butter in microwave at High power 10 to 20 seconds. Stir in sugar, brown sugar and cinnamon. Sprinkle evenly over dough. Roll up dough, along the wide edge like jelly roll. Cut in 14 (or 21) slices. Place on greased baking sheets. Using floured rolling pin, flatten slices. Cover and let rise in a warm place about 30 minutes. Brush with melted butter. Sprinkle with topping of sugar, nuts and cinnamon. Cover with waxed paper and flatten to 6 mm (⅛") thickness with rolling pin.

Bake in preheated 400°F (200°C) oven, for 10 to 12 minutes. Remove from baking sheets immediately and let cool on racks.

Orange Streusel Coffee Cake

The orange flavour permeates this healthy light-textured sweet bread.

	1 loaf pan		2 loaf pans or 1 tube pan	
Dough:				
Whole wheat flour	250 mL	1 cup	500 mL	2 cups
All-purpose flour	250 mL	1 cup	250 mL	1 cup
Sugar	50 mL	¼ cup	75 mL	⅓ cup
Grated orange peel	5 mL	1 tsp	7 mL	1½ tsp
Salt	5 mL	1 tsp	7 mL	1½ tsp
Butter or margarine	25 mL	2 tbsp	35 mL	3 tbsp
Eggs	1	1	2	2
Orange juice	50 mL	¼ cup	75 mL	⅓ cup
Milk	125 mL	½ cup	200 mL	¾ cup
Yeast	7 mL	1½ tsp	10 mL	2 tsp
Topping:				
Brown sugar	175 mL	⅔ cup	250 mL	1 cup
All-purpose flour	35 mL	3 tbsp	50 mL	¼ cup
Cinnamon	15 mL	1 tbsp	25 mL	2 tbsp
Soft butter or margarine	35 mL	3 tbsp	50 mL	¼ cup
Glaze:				
Icing sugar	175 mL	⅔ cup	250 mL	1 cup
Soft butter or margarine	15 mL	1 tbsp	25 mL	2 tbsp
Orange juice concentrate	15 mL	1 tbsp	25 mL	2 tbsp

Prepare dough. If making large recipe, divide dough, topping and glaze in two. Grease pan(s).

Topping: Combine brown sugar, flour, cinnamon and butter.

Knead dough a few times on floured surface and divide in half. Put one half in pan(s); evenly sprinkle with topping. Press remaining dough on top. Brush with oil, cover and let rise in a warm place until doubled, about 20 minutes. Bake in a preheated 375°F(190°C) oven for 25 to 35 minutes or until browned. Remove from pan and let cool on rack about 10 minutes. Place on serving plate.

Glaze: Beat icing sugar, butter and orange juice concentrate together in small bowl; drizzle over cake while still warm, so that it flows down sides.

Bath Buns

The change from raisins to apricots brings these easy-to-make buns, originally from Bath, England, into the 21st century.

	10 Buns		16 Buns	
All-purpose flour	500 mL	2 cups	750 mL	3 cups
Sugar	50 mL	¼ cup	75 mL	⅓ cup
Finely chopped apricots	50 mL	¼ cup	75 mL	⅓ cup
Grated lemon peel	10 mL	2 tsp	15 mL	1 tbsp
Salt	2 mL	½ tsp	5 mL	1 tsp
Mace	1 mL	¼ tsp	2 mL	½ tsp
Margarine or butter	25 mL	2 tbsp	35 mL	3 tbsp
Vanilla	2 mL	½ tsp	5 mL	1 tsp
Egg yolk	1	1	1	1
Milk	200 mL	¾ cup	300 mL	1¼ cups
Yeast	5 mL	1 tsp	7 mL	1½ tsp
Lemon juice	10 mL	2 tsp	15 mL	1 tbsp
Egg white	1	1	1	1
Sugar (coarse, if possible)	25 mL	2 tbsp	35 mL	3 tbsp

Prepare dough. Grease baking sheet(s). Knead dough on floured surface a few times. Divide in 10 (or 16) equal portions and roll as balls between "floured" hands. Space evenly on baking sheet(s). Brush buns with lemon juice, cover and let rise in a warm place until doubled, about 30 minutes.

Beat egg white until thin and brush on buns, then sprinkle with sugar.

Bake in preheated 375°F (190°C) oven 15 to 20 minutes or until browned.

tip: *To prevent sticking, cut apricots with kitchen scissors dipped in flour.*

Danish Pastries

These flaky, melt-in-your mouth treats filled with apricot or raspberry jam are so good. Prepare the dough one day and bake it the next.

	12 to 14 pastries		18 to 21 pastries	
Dough:				
All-purpose flour	500 mL	2 cups	750 mL	3 cups
Sugar	25 mL	2 tbsp	35 mL	3 tbsp
Ground cardamom	5 mL	⅛ tsp	1 mL	¼ tsp
Salt	5 mL	1 tsp	7 mL	1½ tsp
Lemon juice or peel	15 mL	1 tsp	7 mL	1½ tsp
Vanilla	1 mL	¼ tsp	2 mL	¼ tsp
Egg	1	1	1	1
Milk	225 mL	⅞ cup	350 mL	1⅓ cups
Yeast	10 mL	2 tsp	15 mL	3 tsp
Butter or margarine*	125 mL	½ cup	200 mL	¾ cup

*Do not use soft margarine

Prepare dough. If making large recipe, divide dough in half to make handling easier.

Roll butter flat between two sheets of waxed paper, in rectangle about 6 mm (¼") thick for the small recipe (2 rectangles for the large recipe). Wrap butter in waxed paper and refrigerate or freeze if room temperature is warm, until firm.

Choose the fillings from the Fillings section (page 164), and the shape as described on page 163.

On well-floured surface, roll dough in a rectangle about 2 cm (1") wider than slab of chilled butter and three times the length. Place butter in centre of dough and fold over two extending pieces of dough, pressing down on dough to seal in butter. Roll dough out to a rectangle, then fold in thirds and roll in a rectangle again. Repeat folding and rolling twice more. If butter starts to soften, wrap dough in plastic and refrigerate 30 to 40 minutes before proceeding.

Wrap and chill dough for at least 30 minutes or up to 1 week.

Prepare filling, using approximately 15 mL (1 tbsp) filling per pastry.

Grease baking sheets to hold all pastries with room for them to spread. Sprinkle greased sheets with flour, then shake off excess.

Roll dough out on floured surface, as a rectangle 3 cm (⅛") thick and 30 cm (12") wide. Using floured sharp knife, cut in 10 cm (4") squares. Prepare shapes described on page 163.

Preheat oven to 400°F (200°C).

Place cut dough pieces on baking sheet for easier filling.

Brush pastries with beaten egg before baking if shiny surface is desired. Jam is usually added to pastry after baking to give a better appearance. After shaping pastries, cover baking sheet loosely with towel and refrigerate 1 to 2 hours, or overnight, before baking.

Bake 15 to 20 minutes, until puffed and browned. Should pastries open, carefully press them back together while still hot. Cool on a rack.

tip: *If Danish pastries are not light and flaky, let the dough chill in the refrigerator between rolling next time you make them.*

TRADITIONAL DANISH SHAPES

Envelopes:

Put filling in centre, fold corners into centre, slightly overlapping them and firmly press points down.

Pinwheels:

Make diagonal cut, 4 cm (1½") long, from each corner toward centre. Put filling in centre, bring every other point into centre and press down.

Cockscombs:

These are traditionally filled with almond paste. Put filling at centre of one-half of each square and fold in half, pressing edges together. Cut three-quarters of the way toward fold in four places along seam. Curve to open slashes to form cockscomb.

Coffee cake:

Use one small recipe or ⅔ of large recipe. Use remaining dough to make individual pastries.

Grease round cake pan. Cut a circle of dough using bottom of pan as a guide, cutting slightly larger to allow for shrinkage. Fit into bottom of pan. Brush this with a mixture of one egg white beaten with 5 mL (1 tsp) water. Roll remaining dough in square by layering scraps of dough and folding and rolling again. Spread with:

50 mL	(¼ cup)	soft butter
50 mL	(¼ cup)	sugar
10 mL	(2 tsp)	almond extract

Roll up dough and cut in seven pieces and arrange evenly in pan, cut side down.

Cover pan loosely with towel. Refrigerate 1 to 2 hours before baking. Bake in preheated 350°F (175°C) oven for 45 to 50 minutes or until browned.

Drizzle with a thin icing of your choice (page 140).

TRADITIONAL DANISH FILLINGS

Jam:

Apricot and raspberry jam are the most common, however, any jam will be delicious. Jelly may break down with heat, so it is not recommended. Almond and Cheese filling recipes follow.

Almond:

The following 3 versions of Almond filling may be used.

❖ Commercial marzipan may be used as purchased.

❖ 240 g (8 oz) commercial almond paste mixed with 1 egg yolk.

❖ To make marzipan, combine

250	mL	(1 cup) finely ground almonds
125	mL	(½ cup) sugar
1	egg	

Cheese:

250	mL	(1 cup) Ricotta cheese
50	mL	(¼ cup) sugar
10	mL	(2 tsp) grated lemon peel
1	egg yolk	

Combine in bowl, stirring thoroughly.

TREATS FOR FURRY FRIENDS

Never overlook the possibility that baking failures can become pet treats. Some tough over-baked buns may just be the perfect snack and crisp enough to keep a dog's teeth clean. One of my friends made himself very popular with the local squirrels who got my testing failures as their between-nuts treats. Just remember that birds should not be fed bread, since it is not the coarse type of food their digestive system needs.

Here are some special recipes for dogs, but cats have been known to enjoy them as well.

Dog Biscuits Loved By Cats

Ingredient	Metric		Imperial
Whole wheat flour	750	mL	3 cups
Grated cheese*	250	mL	1 cup
Garlic salt	25	mL	2 tbsp
Bacon fat	125	mL	½ cup
Egg	1		1
Milk	250	mL	1 cup

*Choose your pet's favourite. Most dogs love Cheddar.

Put ingredients into bread pan and set on dough cycle. After kneading, the dough is ready to use.

Roll out dough on floured surface to 1 cm (½") thick. Cut in strips 1 x 8 cm (½ x 3") long. Place on ungreased baking sheet(s).

Bake in preheated 350°F (175°C) oven for 30 to 40 minutes or until crisp. Best left in oven to cool and crispen overnight.

Healthy Dog Biscuits

Whole wheat flour	375	mL	1½	cups
Rolled oats	200	mL	¾	cups
Nonfat milk powder	125	mL	½	cup
Soya flour	50	mL	¼	cup
Dog nutrient supplement (oil type)	15	mL	1	tbsp
Cod liver oil	50	mL	¼	cup
Egg	1		1	
Water	250	mL	1	cup

Prepare as in previous recipe. These biscuits can be left in the bread machine until the dough cycle is complete, if you are busy, but is ready to use after kneading is complete.

The aroma of cod liver oil may be strong, so choose a baking day when windows can be opened.

Index